Mental
Strength

Condition your Mind
Achieve your Goals

Iain Abernethy

Published by NETH Publishing
In association with Summersdale Publishers Ltd

Mental Strength

Copyright © Iain Abernethy 2005

First Published by NETH Publishing 2005
Reprinted 2008

NETH Publishing, PO Box 38, Cockermouth, Cumbria, CA13 0GS, United Kingdom. www.iainabernethy.com

In association with Summersdale Publishers Ltd, 46 West Street, Chichester, PO19 1RP, United Kingdom. www.summersdale.com

Printed and Bound in Great Britain by J H Haynes & Co Ltd.

ISBN 0 9538932 4 3

Every effort has been made to obtain the necessary permissions with reference to copyright material, both illustrative and quoted; should there be any omissions in this respect we apologise and shall be pleased to make the appropriate acknowledgements in any future edition.

For David, Rhys and Jenna. Your Dad thinks you're great!

Contents

Introduction

'It's time to start living the life you've imagined'
– Henry James

We all have the potential to achieve anything we wish and to become anything we want to be. To fulfil this potential we need to develop our mental strength so that we are able to push past the obstacles we face as we attempt to improve the quality of our lives. All of us can increase our mental strength through understanding and following a relatively straightforward process. This book will explain that process.

As we leave our old lives behind and begin to pursue our dreams, it is an inescapable consequence that we will feel insecure, scared, filled with self-doubt, experience a lack of confidence or even feel completely overwhelmed by the tasks ahead. If not effectively dealt with, these feelings can make us shrink back from realising our true potential. Feeling unable to move beyond these feelings, we retreat to the unfulfilling comfort of the familiar and everyday. However, it doesn't have to be that way!

To realise our potential we need to develop a mind strong enough to overcome all negative and limiting thoughts. Through reading this book you will learn that negative thoughts and feelings, although unpleasant, are completely natural and with the right mindset they can be used as a positive force that will develop your strength, attributes and talents. Through developing a strong mind, the obstacles and difficulties you face will no longer prevent you from living your life as you truly want to. Rather they will become the path to your success!

Let us be clear from the very start that the path to success is never easy. The notion of effortlessly achieving all the things we want from life is certainly an alluring one. However, that's not the way things are. Growth always involves stepping outside your comfort zone, and therefore by definition involves facing up to uncomfortable situations. In the following chapters I will explain how you can develop the mental strength to effectively deal with, and benefit from, the discomfort of growth.

Whilst some people feel trapped within their current comfort zone, those who understand mental strength find themselves imprisoned by nothing. There is nothing they cannot achieve and nothing they cannot become. This book will show you how to develop mental strength and how to use that strength to achieve all your goals.

Having introduced the nature of this book, I would now like to briefly introduce myself. My name is Iain Abernethy and I make my living as both a professional writer and martial arts instructor. It's a great life!

As a child I was not physically gifted and I was awkward and clumsy. I was also the only child in my school who was deemed to need extra lessons for their writing. Many would have said that the chances of my becoming an able martial artist and a professional writer were slim at best. However, I'm now a fifth dan black belt and one of the United Kingdom's leading exponents of applied karate. I'm also the author of five published books and over fifty magazine articles. I achieved those things by following the process covered in this book; although in the early days not always knowingly. It's not that I'm anything special, it's just that the process works.

As I progressed, the nature of mental strength and the process of developing it became clearer. I better understood not only how to strengthen my mind, but also how to make use of that strength to progress towards my goals. Some time ago I decided to write an article on mental strength for my newsletter. The article subsequently appeared in one of the martial arts magazines I write for and on numerous websites. The response to the article was overwhelming! It's not unusual for me to receive considerable correspondence upon the publication of an article; however the response to that particular article was unprecedented! People were really enthused by it. Around the same time, the prolific author Geoff Thompson had also been encouraging me to write a book of this nature. Geoff has been a huge help to me and his guidance has always been invaluable. So I got to work and wrote the book you are now reading!

I don't write this book as someone who has attained some ultimate level of mental strength; far from it. Rather I write this book as someone who has a good understanding of the process that develops mental strength. It's a method that I have used, and continue to use with much success. Indeed, all the successful people I know make use of this process, even if they don't realise it or describe it as presented here. Although there are many elements to developing mental strength, overall it's a fairly straightforward process that anyone can follow. We can all become as mentally strong as we choose to be.

Before we leave the introduction, I'd like to emphasise that the process of developing mental strength first needs to be understood and then followed up with action. Reading this book is not enough; it's just a first step. You need to understand the process and then act in accordance with it. Through understanding and action you will develop a strong mind. With a strong mind, you will be able to achieve your goals and live your ideal life.

With the introduction over, you've now taken the first step of the first step. Congratulations, you're on your way! Let's now move on to the first chapter and discuss the nature of mental strength.

Chapter 1

What is Mental Strength?

'Shallow men believe in luck.
Strong men believe in cause and effect'
– Ralph Waldo Emerson

In this book we'll be examining the concept of mental strength. We'll be looking at how we can strengthen our minds, and how we can utilise that strength to achieve what we want in life. Before we go any further, we need to clearly define exactly what we mean by mental strength.

We probably all have some definition of strength in our minds, but we will need a common definition that we can work with throughout this book. The dictionary I keep next to my desk defines 'strength' as 'the capability to exert power'. The key part of this definition is the word 'power'. Therefore, to further our understanding of what strength is, we need to more clearly define power. The same dictionary defines power as 'the ability to cause things to happen'. We could therefore define strength as 'the capability to cause things to happen'.

When talking about physical strength, this capability to cause things to happen will manifest itself in physical ways: a weightlifter lifting a large weight, a sprinter setting a new record time, a boxer landing a knockout punch, etc. In these physical examples, the athletes all have the capability to cause things to happen. We would therefore class those athletes as being physically strong.

In this book we are not talking about physical strength, but about mental strength. However, there are many similarities. In all of the preceding examples of physical strength, some kind of resistance was overcome. The weight was difficult for the weightlifter to move, but that resistance was overcome and the weight was lifted. It was difficult for the sprinter to run faster than anyone had ever done previously, but he did. The boxer's opponent was doing his utmost to stop the boxer from winning, but the boxer overcame his opponent's resistance and won the bout. As our sportsmen strived to achieve their goals, something was in their way. There was a resistance.

For strength to manifest itself there is always a resistance to be overcome. The weightlifter can't apply his strength without some weights to lift; the sprinter can't apply his speed without a time to beat; and the boxer can't utilise his punching skills unless he has an opponent to fight.

For our purposes, the dictionary definition is not complete as it contains no mention of resistance. All our athletes used their physical strength to overcome a physical resistance (a weight, a required speed, an opponent). A reasonable definition of physical strength would therefore be 'physical strength is the ability to overcome physical resistance and hence cause things to happen'.

We are now one step away from our definition of mental strength. You'll see as we progress through this book that the human body and mind are inseparably linked. Many of the principles that apply to physical development also hold true for mental development. I think we can therefore define mental strength in the following way:

Mental strength is the ability to overcome mental resistance and cause things to happen.

To make use of this definition, we need to fully understand what is meant by both 'things' and 'mental resistance'.

If mental strength is the ability to overcome mental resistance and cause things to happen, then the 'things' in our definition must be the things we want to happen and the things we want to achieve. In the following chapters we'll look at how important it is to clearly define the things we want. For now it is sufficient to understand that the things we are talking about are the things that you personally wish to achieve in life.

It's important to make it clear that we're talking about the things you want to achieve in life; not the things that others will try to convince you that you want to achieve. It's not about the things that advertising, your friends, your parents, your school, society, the prevailing fashions etc. tell you that you should want. It's about what you truly want to achieve as an individual!

Some people want lots of money; others just want financial security. Some people want a big house in the country; others want to travel around the world. Some people want peace and serenity; others want adrenalin and excitement. We're all individuals and what makes one person very happy will make another miserable.

What we want, and our views on what makes those things desirable, will undoubtedly vary. The key thing is to ensure that we have a clear vision of what things we personally want to achieve (more on this later). Whatever we want from life, there is a gap between deciding what we want and then actually achieving it. The first part of this gap is mental resistance.

So, what is resistance? As we have already discussed, a physical resistance is something that needs to be overcome with physical strength if an athlete is going to achieve the things they want. Because this book is about mental strength, we really need to examine the nature of mental resistance. We'll be expanding and building upon our understanding of mental strength and mental resistance as we progress throughout this book.

However, to get us started let's examine one of the most important and immediate aspects of mental resistance.

I can guarantee that you're already familiar with mental resistance, even if you've never used that specific term before. Ever lounged around in bed when you know you should have been up and about half an hour ago? Ever had an important task to do, and put it off by procrastinating? Ever really wanted to do something, but talked yourself out of it? Yep, me too! The lazy, self-doubting, fearful or negative thoughts that you experience on those occasions are mental resistance.

Mental resistance is the thoughts, feelings and beliefs that stand between you and your goals. It's that negative voice in your head that can prevent you from attempting, and therefore achieving, all the things you want in life. We'll discuss why these thoughts occur and cover their nature and role in the next chapter. For now, all we need to understand is what mental resistance is.

You'd like to try a new activity, but don't begin because you're sure you'll be terrible at it. That negative belief is a form of mental resistance.

You love to sing and would like to eventually turn professional, but you never sing in public because you fear criticism. That fear of criticism is mental resistance.

You've trained hard for a sporting event, but on arriving at the tournament you spot a well-known player and convince yourself that the best you can hope for is second place. Writing yourself off before you even start is mental resistance.

You'd love to apply for your dream job, but you fear that you may not be talented enough to do the actual job, so you don't apply. Feeling that you lack talent and the ability to develop your talents is a form of mental resistance.

Starting to get the idea? Whenever we experience a thought or belief that comes between us and the things we want to achieve, that is mental resistance.

All of the following are examples of mental resistance:

'I'm not talented enough to try that.'

'I'll do it when I've got a bit more money behind me.'

'I'll love to try that, but I'd be embarrassed if I made a mess of it.'

'I'm too old.'

'I'm too young.'

'I'm not clever enough.'

'I'm not skilled enough.'

'People like me don't do that kind of thing.'

'It all seems too complicated for me.'

'I'd love to do that for a living, but I doubt I'd be able to make enough money.'

'I know I could never be as good as they are.'

'I wish I'd taken that up when I was younger; it's too late now.'

'I'm hopeless at that kind of thing.'

'I'm too scared.'

There are some other aspects to mental resistance that we'll cover later on in this book. However, to get us started we can define mental resistance in the following way:

Mental resistance is any negative thought, feeling or belief that stands between you and your goals.

The negative voice of mental resistance can certainly sap our energy and prevent us getting what we want from life. It is therefore quite easy to conclude that mental resistance is inherently bad. However, the paradox is that mental resistance can also help us to achieve our goals!

We're often told that negative thinking is something to be avoided and that we should always ensure our heads are filled with as many positive thoughts as possible. And while that's true, if we are to progress in any area of our lives, it is important that we experience negative thoughts and mental resistance. Confused? That's OK. Things will become a lot clearer in the next chapter.

Chapter 2

Mental Resistance

*'When everything seems to be going against you, remember
that the airplane takes off against the wind, not with it'*
– Henry Ford

In the last chapter we established that mental resistance is
the thoughts and beliefs that stand between us and the things
we want from life. We also discussed that mental resistance is
actually a vital part of ensuring that we achieve those exact
same goals! In this chapter, we'll explain why mental resistance
occurs and why it is vital for our development.

We're probably all familiar with the negative thoughts that
form mental resistance, but the question that needs to be
answered is why these thoughts occur in the first place. And
before we can answer why they occur, we need to understand
when they occur.

Negative thoughts normally arise when you are are in a
situation, or about to attempt something, that your
subconscious, rightly or wrongly, considers risky.

To take an extreme example, let's say that you're about to do
a parachute jump for the first time. You're thousands of feet in
the air, you've never done a parachute jump before, and you're
about to leap out of a perfectly good aeroplane! What thoughts
are likely to be running through your mind? Are you likely to
be thinking these positive, happy thoughts?:

'What a lovely view!'

'This is so much fun!'

'I wish this could last forever!'

Or are the following thoughts more likely to be popping into your head?:

'This is higher than I thought it would be! I'm not sure I can handle this!'

'I'm absolutely terrified; I really want to back out and go back home!'

'I never want to do this ever again!'

Unless you're a very experienced skydiver, I think we can agree that you're probably more likely to be thinking the negative thoughts from the second list. The reason you're much more likely to think those negative thoughts is that your brain considers what you're about to do to be a risk, and hence tries to talk you out of it. So why does the brain do this? The simple answer is survival!

Let's say that your brain actually liked it when you took risks. Instead of trying to talk you out of what it perceived as risky situations, it actually encouraged you to seek them out. How long do you think you'd live?

'Let's leap off this tall building; it will be such a laugh!'

'Let's go pick a fight with that gang over there; they look really dangerous!'

'It would be fun to try to out run that speeding car! I wonder if I could do it? Only one way to find out!'

Through thousands of generations and the process of evolution, we've inherited a brain that tries to talk us out of risky situations. Now, I'm pretty sure that there may have been the odd caveman who simply loved to poke sabre-toothed tigers with pointy sticks, but I'm also sure that they were weeded out of the gene pool pretty quickly!

When it comes to staying alive, the discouraging negative thoughts that prevent us from endangering our lives are very useful and most welcome. We're often told that it's good to face our fears, but there are definitely some fears we shouldn't face! Fear is not always a bad thing. For example, I'd be pretty scared if I was about to leap out of a tree onto a metal spike! Should I confront that fear? I'll give it a miss if it's all the same with you.

The problem we have is that our brains are pretty poor at determining what a real risk is. Ever watched a scary movie and actually felt afraid? You know you're not going to come to any real harm, but the brain still triggers that emotional response. You jump out of your seat (if the movie is any good) and avert your eyes as a socially acceptable way to run away. Ever ridden on a rollercoaster and screamed your lungs out? Again, you're in no real danger, and you know that, but you still feel like you are.

Ever felt terrified before a job interview? You don't have the job now, and the worst that can happen is you make a complete mess of the interview and you still don't have the job. Where's the risk? You could argue that the risk is not getting the job. However, I'm sure you'll agree that you're more likely to get the job if you are calm and collected rather than being a terrified, wobbly mess. The brain mistakes a perceived risk for an actual physical threat and responds accordingly.

When threatened, we call upon the much talked about flight or fight response. As a theory, it's my view that flight or fight is missing an all important third 'f'; that of 'freeze'.

Let's say that one of our caveman ancestors comes across one of the aforementioned sabre-toothed tigers. To survive, he basically has three options: he can run away (flight), he can kill it (fight), or he can remain perfectly still and hope the tiger does not spot him (freeze). His survival instincts will kick in and his brain will prompt him to get out of the situation by one of those three methods. In this situation, assuming he's going to survive, it is likely our caveman will subconsciously think, 'You're not strong enough to kill the tiger. It can easily out run you. So stay still, do nothing, and hope it has not seen you!'

Now it could be argued that the caveman's thoughts are negative (he's told himself that he's slow and weak). However, in that extreme situation his negative thinking saved his life! The sabre-toothed tiger posed a very real threat and had our caveman felt positive about the situation, and not responded to the threat, he could easily have been killed.

Our caveman's first instinct would be to freeze. Had the tiger spotted our caveman and moved towards him, we would hope that the caveman's instincts would now tell him to run. And should running not be possible, he will have no other option but to fight the beast. In all three scenarios, the overriding thought is likely to be, 'You need to get out of this situation… and fast!'

Let's say that a week or so after our caveman successfully avoided the sabre-toothed tiger, he inadvertently strolls near to the location of his close shave. Upon recognising the area, he will feel fear and his brain will discourage him from entering that area. He is very likely to think, 'Don't go any further! If you enter this area bad things could happen. You should quickly turn around and head back the way you came!'

As we've already discussed, for our survival it is very important that we avoid threatening situations and that is why the flight, fight or freeze response feels so unpleasant. If it felt good, we'd all endanger ourselves all the time! When confronted with a risk, our brains set off that negative feeling and the negative thoughts quickly follow in order to encourage us to avoid that risk now and in the future.

We can all agree that being attacked by a wild beast, shot at, physically attacked or being in a building which is on fire are all very real threats to our lives and hence our brains are doing the right thing by encouraging us to get out of that situation in the correct way (flight, fight or freeze). Our brains would also be quite correct in discouraging us from getting into that situation in the first place (negative and discouraging thoughts).

Returning to the perceived threat of the job interview, how relevant is flight, fight or freeze? You could run out of the office screaming (flight), punch the interviewer (fight), or just stay totally silent and motionless throughout the interview (freeze)! I think the likely response would be, 'Don't call us; we'll call you... but first we're phoning security!'

Joking aside, we can see that our primitive survival mechanism is not appropriate for this situation. However, because our brains are unable to differentiate between real and perceived threats, our subconscious still treats the situation as a life-threatening event and invokes the associated response.

Our stone-age brain has not had time to evolve to meet the needs of the modern world. Whilst it is certainly very useful and effective for real life-threatening situations, it overreacts and is overcautious for many of the situations we face in the twenty-first century. By way of example, let's say that you've been asked to give a speech at a social event. This situation is definitely not life-threatening. The worst that can happen is you give a poor speech, you get embarrassed, and some of your friends may make fun of you. However, the threat of making a fool of yourself and being the butt of a few jokes is treated by the brain as a threat to your life! The wholly unpleasant sensation of flight, fight or freeze is evoked and negative thoughts try to persuade you to avoid this 'threatening' situation. You may really want to give the speech, but your stone-age survival response may be able to prevent you from doing so.

So far we have seen that our survival response, although life-saving in the correct situation, can be incorrectly triggered whenever you find yourself in a situation that your brain considers to be threatening. When triggered, our survival response invokes unpleasant feelings, and negative and discouraging thoughts. These feelings and thoughts will need to be dealt with if we are to undertake the task that triggered them. We have previously defined these inappropriate thoughts as mental resistance.

These discouraging thoughts can be pretty convincing and appear in many guises (mental resistance can be pretty sneaky!). Look again at the list on page 15. If we look a little closer at the underlying cause of all the thoughts listed, we can see that all those thoughts really originate from the fact that your survival mechanism considers the task you are about to attempt to be some kind of threat and it would rather you avoided the situation altogether! Now that's OK if the situation is truly life-threatening, but what if the situation, although a little intimidating, is a task we need to undertake in order to achieve the things we want from life?

The logical, more evolved part of your brain knows that speaking in public is not a real threat (embarrassment never killed anyone). However, the survival-based primitive brain is convinced that public speaking is a genuine danger! How does the whole brain make sense of this conflict? The answer is through compromise. The logical part of your brain can't accept 'this is a real threat!' as a believable reason not to do something. However 'You're not talented enough!' could be plausible. It does not have to be true; it just needs to be plausible! The logical part of your brain has a 'reason' not to attempt the task and the survival mechanism is happy because you're now not doing the threatening activity! Your brain has conspired to talk you out of attempting the task (mental resistance has triumphed!).

As we established in chapter one, mental resistance is any negative thought, feeling or belief that stands between you and your goals. Whilst mental resistance can prevent us from attempting to achieve our goals, it is the process of removing and reducing that same mental resistance that makes us capable of achieving them. Everything you want in life lies on the other side of mental resistance. If we want to grow, we need to face up to mental resistance and move beyond it. As we'll see as we progress through this book, the actual process of dealing with mental resistance will bring many benefits! So how do we approach mental resistance? And how do we get past it?

Returning to our example of a speech at a social event, let's say that you've spoken in public many times before and have a good track record of delivering amusing, moving and entertaining speeches. Is the survival response likely to be set off in this situation? No, because you won't perceive the situation as any kind of threat. Your subconscious won't try to talk you out of it and is more likely to actively encourage what it knows from experience will be a rewarding situation. There will be no mental resistance.

From this example, we can see that the level of mental resistance experienced will be directly proportional to the level of the perceived threat. To reduce the level of mental resistance we need to reduce the level of the perceived threat. So how do we do that?

There are three ways to reduce the perceived threat and the associated mental resistance.

Way 1: Don't attempt the threatening activity!

This way is undoubtedly the easiest. If you listen to the inappropriate survival response and decide not to attempt the activity, you avoid the threat. There is no longer any risk and you won't experience any mental resistance. However, whilst this is undoubtedly the most popular method it does have the major drawback of guaranteeing that you'll never achieve your goals. Also, if you decide later that perhaps you'd been a little hasty and you'd like to attempt that activity again, the threat level could be even greater (you've had a failure that could be used to justify the perceived threat) and, therefore, the mental resistance would also be greater. This method only works if we never try to advance ourselves.

Way 2: Compromise your goals.

Let's say that you wanted to be the national champion of your chosen sport. You qualify for the national championships, get the entry form for the event and then the survival mechanism kicks in, 'There will be some really good people at this event and they could make you look pretty stupid in front of a very large crowd! You really shouldn't enter it.' Rather than enter, you decide to permanently aim low and only enter local tournaments. There may still be a perceived threat at these local events, and therefore a small amount of mental resistance. However, in this lower threat environment it will be much smaller than the perceived threat and mental resistance experienced if you had continued to pursue your goal of being national champion.

By compromising our goals, we reduce the threat and therefore the mental resistance experienced, but only if we permanently stay at that lower level. The instant we reach for our true goal, mental resistance will return.

Way 3: Become mentally stronger so that you can overcome the mental resistance.

In the last chapter we defined mental strength as the ability to overcome mental resistance and cause things to happen. Being mentally strong will allow us to overcome the mental resistance caused by a perceived threat. Despite the fact that the activity may intimidate us, we have sufficient mental strength to attempt that activity regardless.

Through overriding the mental resistance and attempting the activity, we will gain experience. The next time we attempt that activity, we will have experience of it, we will have learned a few lessons, and therefore the perceived risk will not be as great. Our survival mechanism now knows from experience that the activity has been successfully confronted in the past and therefore its response will be more moderate. The more experience we have of an activity, the less threatening it becomes.

The key to reducing the perceived threat level, is having the mental strength to overcome the mental resistance induced by the activity and therefore gain experience of that activity. So how do we make ourselves mentally stronger?

You'll remember that on a number of occasions I've said that mental resistance is needed if we are to make progress. And although certain aspects of mental resistance are negative, contrary to much of prevailing thought, we need that negativity in order to make progress. There are some positive aspects to negative thoughts!

One of the positive aspects of mental resistance is the fact that it only appears when you're about to attempt something your survival mechanism perceives as risky. If you were to live your life exactly as you do now, and never attempt anything new, your survival mechanism is unlikely to ever be triggered. The appearance of mental resistance is a good indicator that you're about to do something quite special. Every time you take a step towards achieving the things you want in your life, mental resistance will be in front of you encouraging you to turn back! This means that we can use mental resistance as a guide to which way to go. Just head towards the mental resistance and you're more likely to be on the path to all the things you want!

Now this news may be discouraging for some. We all know that mental resistance does not feel nice, and perhaps some of you were hoping this book would give you a way to avoid those feelings. Sorry to disappoint you, but those feelings will always be there as long as you're doing things to improve the quality of your life. There is no such thing as effortless and discomfort-free progress! Experiencing mental resistance, although unpleasant, means that your life is about to get better! We do, of course, need to get past that resistance in order to walk the path towards our ideal life, and as we've already covered, we need mental strength to do that.

To develop physical strength, we need some form of physical resistance to overcome. As a keen weightlifter since my teens, I know that to get stronger I need to lift weights that cause me some discomfort. By attempting to overcome that physical resistance and the associated discomfort, my body will adapt and become physically stronger. Our minds work in a similar way.

To become mentally stronger, we need a mental resistance to overcome. The great thing is that mental resistance automatically appears whenever we head towards our goals! The negative thoughts and mental resistance that appear when we move towards our goals will actually help to give us the mental strength needed to achieve those goals! How cool is that! The fact that mental resistance can also make us stronger is another one of its positive attributes.

It is important to understand that anything that requires strength also has the ability to develop strength. Lifting weights requires physical strength, and lifting weights also has the ability to develop strength. Likewise, overcoming mental resistance requires mental strength, and overcoming mental resistance will develop mental strength!

This may seem like a bit of a paradox at first: we need mental strength to overcome mental resistance but we need mental resistance in order to develop mental strength! However, it only seems paradoxical because we have not yet covered exactly how we make use of mental resistance in order to develop the strength of our minds.

When developing physical strength, we need a structured and scientific training programme if we are to make progress in a safe and effective way. If you just ran into the nearest gym and started trying to lift the heaviest weights in the place, you are unlikely to get stronger and are very likely to injure yourself. You need to understand how to perform the various exercises and learn the key training principles that will allow you to make steady progress. It is exactly the same with mental strength. In chapter three we'll discuss the key 'training principle' that will allow you to develop your mental strength, overcome mental resistance, and make positive and real progress towards all the things you want in life.

Not only does facing up to mental resistance have the capability to develop mental strength, the same process can also develop our talents! An increase in talent will also help us to achieve the things we want in life. We'll discuss how this works later on in this book. For now, it is enough to understand that although mental resistance can prevent us from attempting to change our situation, if we face up to that mental resistance it can be a positive force that will provide all the things we need to achieve our goals.

Before we move on, it is important to review some of the key points raised in this chapter.

Mental resistance appears whenever you are about to attempt something that your subconscious (rightly or wrongly) considers risky. Our primitive survival response is unable to differentiate between real life-threatening events and many of the perceived threats that we experience in the modern world. Our brains attempt to dissuade us from engaging in activities that are perceived as threats, even though engaging in those activities will improve the quality of our lives. This knowledge should therefore lead us to understand that experiencing mental resistance is a good indication that your life is about to improve, providing you don't turn back and have the mental strength to overcome that mental resistance. Although we need mental strength to overcome mental resistance, we also need mental resistance to develop mental strength. At this point, this may seem like a paradox, but only because we have yet to cover the details of the process, and we'll be covering the key principle of this process in the next chapter.

Chapter 3

Overload

'Our strength increases in proportion to the obstacles imposed upon it'
– Paul De Rapin

The key concept relating to the development of mental strength is that of overload. To become physically stronger our muscles need to experience resistances greater than those normally encountered. In practise that means we need to lift weights that are heavier than the weights we are used to. We need to overload the muscle.

For the muscle to overcome this greater than normal resistance, it will need to contract harder than it normally does. The effects of this contraction will stimulate changes within the body that will cause the muscle to become stronger and more able to deal with contractions of that level in the future. Our minds work in a very similar way.

To enable us to become mentally stronger we need to experience resistance greater than that normally encountered. As I've mentioned previously, mental resistance will automatically appear every time we move outside our current comfort zone and attempt to achieve our goals. The very fact that we are attempting something that we do not normally do means that the resistance will be greater than that normally encountered.

Having established that the resistance is easy enough to come across, how can we approach that resistance in a way that will make us stronger and move us towards our goals? How do we address the apparent paradox that we need mental strength to overcome mental resistance, and yet it is mental resistance that develops mental strength?

The best way to explain that there is actually no paradox is to return to the parallels between physical and mental strength. At the time of writing, I can comfortably bench-press (a weight training exercise) ninety kilograms ten times in a row. If I went to the gym and kept lifting ninety kilograms, the physical resistance (weight) is not a resistance greater than that normally encountered. I can lift that weight that many times with relative ease, and therefore the weight is not great enough to make me physically stronger. I'm strong enough to deal with that weight already.

I know that in order to become stronger my muscles need to experience a resistance they do not normally encounter. They have encountered ninety kilograms over a ten-repetition set on many occasions, so I need to lift a heavier weight. However, if I were to place three-hundred kilograms on the bar (a weight my body is certainly not used to experiencing), I'm not physically strong enough to lift that weight. Indeed, if I were to try and lift that weight (and for the record I'm not that stupid!), the attempt could easily result in injury. Far from developing my physical strength, that large a weight could actually make me weaker as my damaged muscles would certainly not be as strong as the healthy ones I now possess.

Returning to mental strength, if we live our lives exactly as we do now, no additional mental resistance will be experienced. Therefore, we have no opportunity to develop our mental strength.

The level of mental resistance we experience when undertaking a task is always directly proportional to how far beyond our current comfort zone that task is. If the task undertaken is within our comfort zone, there will be no resistance and hence no opportunity to develop (a bit like a weightlifter with no weight to lift). If you were to suddenly leap way beyond the edges of your comfort zone, the mental resistance experienced would be too great.

If you increase the mental resistance you experience in a sudden and dramatic way, you'd be trying to cope with levels of resistance your mind is not ready for. In physical terms, this is similar to our example of going from lifting ninety kilograms to attempting to lift three hundred kilograms. This type of shock overload will not increase your mental strength, but is very likely to stress you to the extremes and could easily result in a weakened mental state.

A couple of examples may help to make this concept a little clearer. Let's say that an actress has done some work with her local drama group. She is pretty comfortable working with that group and confident of her ability to act at that level. If she continues where she is, there will be no mental resistance (she is not moving outside her comfort zone) and therefore will have no opportunity to develop her mental strength. There is a lot of wisdom in the phrase, 'If you do what you've always done, you'll get what you've always got.' However, if the actress was to suddenly quit her day job, move to Hollywood and start trying to make her living as a movie star, the mental resistance she would experience would be extreme to say the least!

The stresses and strains of such a bold move are likely to take a heavy toll on the actress. Having never done any film work before, she is unlikely to have the talent to get into films at this level. How is she going to make enough money to support herself? When the money runs out, where will she live? The actress will not become mentally stronger as a result of this much mental resistance. She is likely to find herself unable to cope and is likely to find that the stress of it all makes her mentally weaker.

To develop my physical strength I need to attempt to lift weights that are just beyond what I can comfortably lift. If we were to put a figure on it, I'd say five to ten percent more, depending upon how comfortable the lift is. I should therefore be trying to lift around one-hundred kilograms (which is what I currently do). Attempting to lift that amount of weight is a strain, but I can handle that weight safely. If the weight is too light I won't get stronger. If it is too heavy I run the risk of injury. The key is to lift a weight that is just beyond what I can comfortably manage. Lifting this weight will be uncomfortable, but it is within the realms of achievability. The amount of weight used should not be an easy lift, nor should it be an impossible task. The correct amount of weight will be just enough to cause me to struggle. I call this range the 'zone of development'.

Through lifting a weight that falls within my zone of development, I will strain my muscles just enough to promote an increase in physical strength. The increased weight eventually becomes what I normally encounter and, therefore, there will come a point when the increased weight is easy to lift and it will no longer develop my strength. Eventually that weight will be absorbed into my comfort zone and I'll have to lift a little more to ensure I remain in my zone of development.

From a mental strength perspective, I need to reach just beyond my current comfort zone in order to experience the right amount of mental resistance. Experiencing mental resistance will inevitably result in discomfort. However, at that level I should have sufficient mental strength to keep working through the discomfort until the task becomes what I'm normally accustomed to. This is the answer to the apparent paradox of overcoming resistance requiring strength, and the development of strength requiring resistance. It's simply a matter of exposing ourselves to the right level of resistance. When we are in the zone of development, we will be overloaded and will experience mental resistance, but we will have just enough mental strength to work through it.

By remaining in the zone of development, the mental resistance we experience for any given task will eventually subside. In overcoming this mental resistance, we will have become mentally stronger and our zone of development will have expanded. To grow further, we'll need to further increase the mental resistance we experience by again shifting outside what has become the new comfort zone.

Let's take the example of someone who wants to be an actor. Initially, they've never acted before and, therefore, any attempt at acting will cause mental resistance (self-doubt, stage fright, embarrassment etc.). However, doing exercises with their local drama group overloads our actor by just the right amount. By engaging in the exercises the actor becomes mentally stronger, the resistance will subside, and they will eventually need to take on minor roles in local plays in order to grow yet further. Again, this will cause mental resistance, but the actor will now have the mental strength to work through this increased level of resistance. The actor will become stronger and the mental resistance will again eventually subside. It will then be time to take on leading roles, and so on. If the aspiring actor had attempted to take on a lead role right from the start, the mental resistance experienced would have pushed the actor outside his zone of development. He will not have the mental strength to work through that much resistance and therefore the experience will not result in any growth.

The key to developing our mental strength, and expanding our capabilities, is to keep moving outside our comfort zone into our zone of development. If we move too far outside our comfort zone, such that we overshoot our zone of development, the mental resistance experienced will be too great. This will be extremely stressful and is unlikely to develop our mental strength. Ensuring that we don't over shoot the zone of development is very important, and again we find many parallels with physical training.

When we are in our physical zone of development, our muscles will be working hard and therefore producing significant quantities of lactic acid. It is this acid which causes the burning sensation associated with strenuous exercise. An experienced weightlifter will be able to use the intensity of that burning sensation to judge if they are within their zone of development or not. If a weightlifter were to stop the instant they felt the beginnings of that burning sensation, they're unlikely to stress the muscle enough to stimulate an increase in physical strength. Likewise, if you return to your comfort zone at the first sign of a little mental resistance, you won't develop your mental strength and will become imprisoned by your comfort zone.

The muscles have a built-in mechanism to discourage you from working so hard that you damage them. As you work towards the upper levels of your zone of development, the lactic acid in the muscles will increase to the point where it will chemically and physically interfere with the function of the muscle. The muscle won't move as easily and you get that intense burning feeling in the affected muscles. Weightlifters refer to this point as 'failure' and use it a sign to stop working the affected muscle (at least until it's had a little rest). Working until failure is one of the key concepts of physical development as it guarantees you are at the upper end of your zone of development.

Once the muscle has been worked to its limit, the experienced weightlifter knows they have stressed their muscle exactly the right amount to stimulate an increase in strength and they will cease the exercise. Any attempts to work the muscles yet further, would not only be futile, but would also be counterproductive and likely to result in injury. To develop the maximum amount of physical strength within an efficient timescale, we need to work to the upper limits of our zone of development, but not go beyond that zone. Mentally we have to approach things in a very similar way.

As we've already covered, our minds also have a zone of development. But unlike our muscles, our minds do not have such a straightforward mechanism to let us know when we're running the risk of moving beyond that zone of development. However, just like a weightlifter, we need to keep a close eye on ourselves and analyse how we feel in order to ensure we remain in the zone of development and don't overdo it.

In the development of physical strength, there is a concept called overtraining. Overtraining is when we push our bodies so hard that they start to break down and training becomes counterproductive. There is a fine line between training at the limit of your zone of development and running yourself into the ground! One of the other effects of overtraining is a dwindling enthusiasm for training. You may still force yourself to train, but it's a chore and usually far from productive. The drop in enthusiasm and physical stress that accompanies physical overtraining have mental counterparts should we find ourselves outside our mental zone of development.

If you find yourself feeling excessively stressed and you are losing enthusiasm for your goals, there is a strong possibility that you are exposing yourself to too much mental resistance and are outside your zone of development. If this happens, you need to ease off the throttle that little bit so you return to the zone of development. You'll then grow your mental strength and regain enthusiasm for your goals.

When I first decided that I wanted to write, I went through the process of moving into my zone of development. I'd always had a great love of books, but I did not have a great deal of confidence in my ability to write. As a child I really struggled with both handwriting and spelling. In fact, both of them are still awful to this day! In junior school I was given extra lessons by the teachers (the ones who cared) and I was the only child made to write in pencil (to ease the correcting of the numerous mistakes) when my fellow pupils were all allowed to write in pen. These early experiences did little to convince me of my ability to write!

Throughout secondary school I was also constantly criticised for my bad handwriting and poor spelling. I have to be honest and say that I didn't always do my utmost to correct my failings. I'd always really enjoyed writing, but it kind of irritated me that some of my teachers could not see past my presentation to the actual content of my work. As a teenager, I found it infuriating that presentation was valued over content. Whether that was the case or not, that's how I saw it at the time. Some teachers would read what I'd written and then give me constructive feedback. For those teachers I always made the effort. For the ones who only ever wrote 're-do' on my books, I'd normally re-do it with even less care, and so on, until they relented. In case you haven't noticed, I was a pretty stubborn teenager!

After numerous failed exams and years of being told I couldn't write, my comfort zone for writing was pretty small. However, I'd always wanted to write and that meant I had to move outside that comfort zone. When I finally made the firm resolution to become a writer, the first thing I did was buy a cheap word-processor. With one purchase I overcame all my handwriting and many of my spelling problems (spell checkers are wonderful things!). However, I still had little confidence in my ability to write. As soon as I put fingers to keyboard, mental resistance would appear and tell me that I was wasting my time and that I'd never be able to produce work that people would actually want to read.

In order to limit the mental resistance to a manageable level (be in the zone of development) I started out by writing articles with no intention of ever trying to get them published. I wrote a number of what I still consider to be reasonable pieces. However, I'm sad to say that I retreated to the comfort zone and never really moved beyond that point for a number of years.

A few years later, with renewed enthusiasm, and having become very comfortable writing for myself, I started writing my first book (a martial arts instruction book). As the book progressed, I knew that I needed to get better known in the martial arts world if the book was to sell in any significant number. This would inevitably mean getting my work published in the martial arts press. I decided to start sending some of the articles I'd written to the martial arts magazines. Again, mental resistance appeared. By that time, I had more of an appreciation that the appearance of mental resistance was not a reason to retreat but instead meant that I was making progress and was in the zone of development.

A number of the articles were returned and this again gave me an opportunity to grow (improve my work and have the mental strength to get over the rejection and keep on going). Eventually I did get a couple of articles published and the martial arts press have been extremely supportive ever since.

The publication of the book also proved problematic with numerous rejections. Having come this far, and determined not to slip back into the comfort zone, I eventually decided to publish the book myself. This decision also brought with it a great deal of mental resistance: 'What do you know about publishing? You can't afford to risk that much money! If the experienced publishers don't want it, perhaps it's because the book is no good.'

Again, I moved step by step into the zone of development. Firstly, I bought and read a few books on the publishing process. I began to feel relatively comfortable that I understood the basics of the process and decided that it was time to get in touch with people in the business and put my plan into action.

I took it all step by step and my first book was published in October 2000 in association with Summersdale Publishers (a book which still sells well and has now been translated into other languages).

Armed with my increased knowledge of the process, and the profits from the first book, I set about writing more books. Producing each and every one of those books expanded my zone of development. Indeed, with my fourth book, I stepped outside my comfort zone into the world of typesetting and was able to layout and prepare the book for printing to professional standards.

Just before the publication of my fourth book, I quit my day job and took up writing full-time. Leaving a well-paid, steady job for the uncertainty of the life as a full-time writer also brought its share of mental resistance. However, I'd developed my mental strength to the point where I could take that big step and hence remain in the zone of development.

By gradually overcoming mental resistance, becoming mentally stronger and moving outside my comfort zone into the zone of development, the only boy in my school who needed extra lessons for writing had became a professional writer! It's not that I'm anything special; it's just that the process works! You can be whatever you want to be and achieve whatever you want to achieve, so long as you leave your comfort zone, overload yourself just the right amount and keep venturing into the zone of development.

The key to growing your mental strength is overloading yourself just enough. But you do need to overload yourself! There are many people who want things in life, but who are not prepared to overload themselves in order to progress.

It's also an inescapable truth that overloading yourself causes some discomfort. Therefore, if there is no discomfort, there can be no growth. You need to thoroughly internalise this concept so that when you do experience discomfort and mental resistance, you know that it is a sure sign that you're on your way to achieving all the things you want from life. That thought alone can make the discomfort of growth a lot more palatable. We'll discuss discomfort in more detail in chapter five.

In this chapter we have talked about the need to overload ourselves by just the right amount in order to stimulate a development in mental strength. Once we become mentally stronger we are then able to move even closer towards our goals. However, overloading ourselves is not enough; we need to overload ourselves on a consistent basis. We will discuss the importance of consistency in the following chapter.

Chapter 4

The Importance of Consistency

'If we are facing in the right direction,
all we have to do is keep on walking'
– Buddhist Proverb

In the previous chapter, we discussed how we need to move beyond our comfort zone and into our zone of development so that we can develop our mental strength and make progress towards our goals. However, simply overloading ourselves is not enough; we need to do it consistently.

You wouldn't expect to go to the gym only once a month and get fit. Likewise we should not expect to become mentally stronger or achieve the things we want from life with occasional sporadic efforts. If we are to achieve our goals, then we need to be consistent in our efforts to achieve them. We need to move outside our comfort zone to be consistently in our zone of development.

Our bodies and minds are highly adaptable and we will always adapt to the environment in which we place ourselves. If we consistently place ourselves in challenging environments, then the adaptation will be positive. We will become stronger, more confident, more talented and in control of our lives. Conversely, if we shy away from challenges and consistently place ourselves in more comfortable environments, we will adapt in a negative way. We will become mentally weaker and we will find ourselves at the mercy of circumstance.

To develop our mental strength we need to be consistently outside our comfort zone. Mental strength, like physical strength, is reversible. By reversible I mean that just as it is possible to become mentally stronger, it is also possible to become mentally weaker. If we return to the comfort zone and stay there, over time we will get mentally weaker. In fact, the further we retreat into the comfort zone, the weaker we will become.

The temptation to return to the comfort zone is always there. After all, the comfort zone is pretty comfortable! However, the comfort zone has the ability to weaken us and reduce our potential. It's not a place we should dwell in for any length of time.

As a full-time writer, a job that I really love, there are days when I momentarily long for the time when I had a day job. All I had to do was turn up, do my bit and I'd collect my pay at the end of the month. However, I found my old job dull and unfulfilling compared to the excitement and satisfaction of doing something I have a real passion for. To advance my career as a writer, I constantly have to move outside my comfort zone into my zone of development. Being in the zone of development is not comfortable, and, in my weaker moments, I occasionally long for a bit of comfort. My old job, although very unfulfilling, was placed smack bang in the middle of my comfort zone and afforded comfort aplenty. In these weaker moments, I need to flex my mental strength and remind myself that the easy life is hugely unfulfilling, and being in the zone of development, although inevitably challenging and at times uncomfortable, is very satisfying, hugely rewarding and generally a lot of fun!

The comfort zone is comfortable and the zone of development is not. That is why we all get tempted to remain in, or return to, the comfort zone. When this happens, we need to flex our mental strength and then drive ourselves forwards once again.

There is never any advancement without facing up to challenges and dealing with discomfort. It is for this reason that the vast majority of people never fulfil their dreams or achieve their goals. They want the success, but they avoid challenges and the very notion of discomfort. Far from avoiding challenges and discomfort, we need to actively seek them out if we are to develop ourselves and achieve our goals. The right level of discomfort is good for us. And whilst it may seem like a paradox to some, comfort is actually bad for us! There is no quick fix. Only consistently being in the zone of development will bring true advancement. There is no other easier way.

Whatever your goals and ambitions, you can be sure you are making real progress if you feel challenged on a consistent basis. Whenever things are plain sailing then you can be equally assured that you're not where you need to be. Nor are you doing the things you need to do in order to progress.

Whenever I'm practising the martial arts, it has to be a challenge and it has to involve some degree of discomfort. If the training session doesn't stretch me to my limits, then I'm unlikely to gain from it. If I have a few easy sessions in a row, my skills, my physical fitness and my mental resolve will all start to deteriorate. It is only through consistently exposing myself to challenging training that I'll be able to advance. It is the same with any other endeavour. To make progress we need to overload ourselves and we need to do it consistently.

Having emphasised the need to overload ourselves on a regular basis, the next statement may seem contradictory (it isn't): To ensure we progress quickly and safely, we also need to rest! It may seem like I'm contradicting myself here, but you do need to ensure you have a balance between overload and recuperation. Consistently being in the zone of development does not mean we should spend every waking moment in pursuit of our goals.

To help clear up any apparent contradiction, imagine a weightlifter that spends hours in the gym every single day. He's lifting the right amount of weight (in his zone of development) and no one can say he's not being consistent! However, he's not resting. Sooner or later he's going to run out of energy. His muscles won't have time to recover from training before he's training again! Our weightlifter is chronically overtraining.

In order to achieve your goals, you'll need plenty of energy; and as you progress towards those goals, you'll expend that energy. So you need to take a productive rest every now and again in order to restore your energy levels and continue to make worthwhile progress.

A productive rest is not to be confused with returning to the comfort zone. In our weaker moments it is possible to confuse the two, either intentionally or unintentionally. A desire to return to the comfort zone is based upon an unwillingness to endure the discomfort and challenges that always accompany progress. A productive rest is a momentary respite from the stresses of the zone of development so that we can replenish our energy and get right back into the zone of development with maximum effect!

In military terms, a return to the comfort zone is to surrender. A productive rest is a tactical retreat preceding a strong forward push. A productive rest is a very positive activity that is a vital part of the developmental process. Certainly we don't want to spend too much time away from the zone of development or we will weaken and we lose the opportunity to make progress. However, we also don't want to push ourselves so hard that we drain all our energy, as that will also weaken us.

When I'm writing, I find I reach a point, normally after a couple of hours, where to continue writing would be counterproductive. My energy starts to wane and the quality of my writing falls as a result. When I reach this point, I take a productive rest. I go for a quick walk, have something to eat, run a few errands, even watch a bit of TV, anything that gives me a little break from writing for half an hour or so. I can then return to my writing with more energy and renewed enthusiasm.

If I've been working hard for a few days, I sometimes find myself at my desk feeling tired and with little enthusiasm to write or progress my business. That's a sign that I need a productive rest. Sometimes that rest will take the form of playing a few games with my children. Sometimes I'll go and read a book. Sometimes I'll do a bit of extra training, and sometimes I'll go to bed and sleep for an hour or two! The change in activity allows me to recharge my batteries and make strong progress upon returning to the task at hand.

Any experienced athlete knows that they need to consistently push their boundaries if they are to become physically stronger and enhance their physical skills. However, they also know the value of rest. In order to push their limits, they need maximum energy. The only way to gain that energy is through sufficient rest.

It isn't wise to wait until you're burnt out until you decide that you need to rest. What you should do is plan your advancement so that your productive rests are a built-in part of the process. There is nothing wrong with giving yourself a little time off so long as you're doing so for positive reasons. Productive rests are a vital part of the developmental process and should never be confused with laziness! That said, you should also never try to justify laziness by trying to convince yourself and others that you're just resting.

To make meaningful progress we need to be in the zone of development on a consistent basis. In order to make that possible, we need to ensure we get enough rest. The instant our energy levels are restored, we need to get back into the zone of development and use that energy to progress ourselves towards our goals.

Being in the zone of development is hard work. However, there may also be other reasons that can cause us to be inconsistent with our efforts to develop. These reasons for inconsistency – which aren't valid reasons at all – can include things like boredom, a lack of progress, self-doubt gaining a foothold etc. We'll discuss these prompts to inconsistency in more detail as we progress through this book. However, for now, the key thing to understand is that to make meaningful progress we need to be consistent in our efforts. We will take productive rests to make sure we have maximum energy, but we won't reside in the comfort zone, nor will we try to justify inconsistent effort.

As we covered earlier, the main reason that most people are inconsistent in their efforts is that the zone of development is an uncomfortable place to be. However, as we'll discuss in the next chapter, discomfort is very necessary for our growth.

Chapter 5

The Necessity of Discomfort

*'Every step forward is made at the cost of
mental and physical pain'*
– Friedrich Nietzsche

One of the recurring themes in the preceding chapters is the necessity of discomfort. Without a resistance to overcome, we have no way of getting stronger. The process of leaving our comfort zone behind and moving into the zone of development invariably means that mental resistance will be present. The presence of mental resistance, and the overcoming of mental resistance, is always uncomfortable. Because we need to overcome mental resistance in order to make any kind of progress, we can therefore see that progress is always accompanied by discomfort.

For some readers, that may be unwelcome news as the vast majority of people want discomfort-free progress. Unfortunately, there is no such thing. If there is no discomfort, then there is no progress. However, the idea of discomfort-free progress is an alluring one.

I have a few questions for you. Do you know anyone who has a washboard stomach who trains for five minutes a day? Nope, me neither. Anyone I know who has that level of physical development got there through regular intense physical activity and a very strict diet. But that does not stop innumerable advertisements that promise to make you into the next Mr Universe or give you the figure of a top model in only a few minutes a day. Somebody must be buying these 'revolutionary' plans and pieces of equipment, if only in order to pay for all of the glossy advertisements. People are very attracted to the false idea that they can achieve great results with mediocre effort and no discomfort.

Do you personally know anyone who became a millionaire by answering an advertisement or an email? I doubt it, but once again we see many advertisements and emails of that nature. I got three such emails this morning! Apparently, I've won two lotteries and there is a foreign dignitary who wants to give me millions of dollars! Whilst such emails are obviously scams, they must work to some degree. Otherwise they wouldn't keep appearing in so many inboxes! The reason they work is that they appeal to the desire to get something for nothing. I hate to be the one to burst bubbles (I don't really!) but progress will always involve discomfort.

Some of the apparent exceptions to this rule are the recipients of good fortune. However, just getting a lucky break will not lead to long-term progress or happiness. Those who find themselves having greatness thrust upon them have to quickly adapt to their new position otherwise they won't be there for long. It's for similar reasons that many lottery winners find themselves deflated a few months after their win. From an average income they find themselves having to switch to the lifestyle of the very rich overnight. This change can fling lottery winners way outside their comfort zone, which is why some lottery winners find themselves wishing they'd never won in the first place!

Any meaningful and sustainable progress will be accompanied by discomfort. However, there is a vast difference between unnecessary pain and growing pain.

Unnecessary pain is the discomfort we experience that brings us no opportunity to strengthen ourselves or grow. There can be no doubt that moving outside the comfort zone is a scary

47

and uncomfortable experience. Indeed, it can be so intimidating to some that, despite a token desire to advance, they will do whatever they can to stay within the comfort zone, even if that involves making the comfort zone uncomfortable!

By adopting a victim mentality we can blame other people, our lot in life, the fact we can't get the breaks and so on for our current situation. We convince ourselves that we are victims of circumstance and hence are unable to move forwards. We may not like where we are, and we may feel uncomfortable and unhappy about our lot in life, but we accept it as our inescapable fate. In short, we adopt a position where we believe that what happens to us is not our responsibility. The cold hard fact is that your life is your responsibility!

To be clear, I'm not saying that other people and situations outside your immediate control can't cause problems for you, or that these problems are somehow all your own doing. What I'm saying is that you do have a choice in whether to let these things hold you back or not. History is full of examples of people who had everything stacked against them and yet they simply refused to accept no for an answer. Nothing could hold them back! There is no reason at all why you can't be one of those people.

To advance we need to take full responsibility for our situation and then attack the bits of that situation that we don't like with full force! The aim is always to court discomfort in order to get past it. In this way we strengthen ourselves and make progress towards our goals. We should never wallow in discomfort. This aimless discomfort is in no way beneficial. It should never be confused with the necessary discomfort that accompanies positive action.

When we adopt the victim mentality we ensure that we can't move beyond our current situation. If our situation isn't anything to do with us, what can we do to change it?! Whilst this mindset persists, we imprison our potential. And for some that's a worthwhile trade-off as it means that things will stay exactly as they are. There are no scary trips outside the comfort zone.

We may not like our situation, and therefore we will be uncomfortable with it, but at least it is familiar. All the discomfort caused by and related to the victim mentality won't bring about any increase in mental strength or any progress.

How many times have you heard people say 'I'd truly love to do that, but I don't have the time… I don't have the money… my husband / wife won't support me… I'll wait until my kids are older… I'll wait until I'm fitter… I'll wait until I'm more confident… I'll wait until I've got more free time, etc.'? The truth is that all statements of this type are underwritten by a fear of moving outside the comfort zone. They are just one more form of mental resistance. Don't get me wrong. Some of the concerns expressed may have some validity, but the refusal to look for ways to address these concerns, other than remaining static, is a sure indicator that the victim mentality is in full effect. If you really want to achieve something, then you will do so, regardless of circumstance. You're only a victim if you choose to be one.

If we adopt the victim mentality we push the things we truly want from life beyond our reach. It can be truly heartbreaking to think that you'll never live life the way you want to. The victim mentality can cause us lots of pain and discomfort. However, all of that pain is unnecessary. We can all achieve the things we want if we choose to step outside the comfort zone and face all challenges and obstacles head on.

By accepting responsibility for our lives we will avoid the unnecessary discomfort of the victim mentality, but we can never escape the discomfort that arises whenever we face up to mental resistance and move outside our comfort zone. As I sit here typing this, my legs are extremely sore as a result of the intense training over the last three days. As a result of that training, my legs will become stronger. The discomfort I'm currently experiencing is a vital part of the strengthening process. If I'd attempted to avoid that discomfort and took it easy, or didn't train at all, I'd deny myself the opportunity to make progress.

It's not that the discomfort itself advances us; it's the process of facing up to that discomfort and then overcoming it that ensures we become mentally stronger and more able to live our lives as we choose. Because advancement is always accompanied by discomfort, the presence of discomfort is a good sign that you're advancing!

All successful people understand that discomfort is a sign of progress, and are therefore not averse to seeking out discomfort or experiencing growing pains. Because the majority of people prefer to remain firmly within their comfort zone, they are not successful. It is this tolerance of discomfort, more than anything else, which separates the successful from the unsuccessful. It's not that successful people are lucky or a different breed. It's simply the fact they are prepared to walk the road less travelled. And it's a road we can all travel.

The initial discomfort we feel when we start to advance outside our comfort zone is not permanent. The very act of willingly stepping into the zone of development guarantees that we will become mentally stronger. By becoming stronger, we are more able to deal with the new tasks and situations, and therefore the discomfort starts to subside. What we must then do, if further progress is to be made, is to reach out yet further.

I know that for some the idea of continually seeking out discomfort is not an attractive one. However, the discomfort associated with growth and advancement is not as unpleasant as it may first sound. As you grow and advance towards your goals, you'll undoubtedly begin to relish the associated discomfort as you begin to appreciate that discomfort always precedes a breakthrough. Discomfort will become the travel companion who is always there to remind you that you're growing stronger and making true progress.

You'll also find that your self-esteem grows when you find yourself willingly courting discomfort. You're the kind of person who goes out there and makes things happen! I guarantee that you'll feel proud of yourself for pushing your boundaries and taking on the associated discomfort. And when that inevitable discomfort arrives, far from wishing to avoid it, you'll want to face it head on as you know for a fact it means that success is on its way.

Does the idea that you'll start to enjoy discomfort seem unlikely to you? It won't once you've got your first few successes under your belt and you've actually experienced the process.

I've been involved in the martial arts since I was a child. For decades it has been a normal part of my life to push my body to extremes on a regular basis. I also spend a great deal of time around fellow martial artists who do likewise. One thing we all acknowledge is that hard training is lots of fun... when it's over! The actual training itself is generally very unpleasant. However, upon the completion of the training, you feel very proud of yourself for pushing yourself that far. You also appreciate that as a direct result of that training, you're now a better martial artist.

Once you've trained for a sufficient length of time, the hard training – although every bit as physically and mentally demanding – actually starts to become enjoyable in a strange kind of way. It's still very unpleasant, but you know you're going to feel great when you've finished. You also know with total certainty that the training is making you a better martial artist. As strange as it may sound to some, you actually start wanting the training to be as hard as possible because it's that kind of training that's the most beneficial and rewarding. You feel cheated if you're not pushed to your limits. It's not that you enjoy the discomfort as such; more that you enjoy what the discomfort leads to. You begin to see discomfort as a necessary means to a glorious end. The discomfort becomes part of the enjoyment process. I'm sure you'll find the same as you pursue you own goals.

To summarise, discomfort is a necessary part of the advancement process. By avoiding discomfort, we are unable to advance. The aim is not to revel in discomfort but to get past it in order to move towards the goals we've set for ourselves. If you accept that discomfort is always going to be part of growth, and you're prepared to endure and overcome that discomfort, then there is nothing that will stand in your way.

Chapter 6

You Are What You Think

'If you think you can do a thing,
or think you can't do a thing, you're right'
– Henry Ford

In the world of physical exercise the phrase 'you are what you eat' is often recited. There is certainly much truth in that statement. The things we take into our bodies make up our bodies. If we eat rubbish, our health will suffer. Conversely, if we eat healthily, we will become healthier.

In the same way that the things that we allow inside our body affect our physical health and strength, the thoughts that we allow inside our minds also affect our mental health and strength. If we allow weak thoughts into our minds, our minds become mentally weaker. If we think strong thoughts, we become mentally stronger.

We all have an image of ourselves within our minds. We have a view on what we are good at, what we are poor at, whether we are outgoing or reserved, whether we are a success or a failure, whether we are strong or weak, and so on. This self-image forms a kind of master plan that will govern our feelings and behaviour in any given situation. For example, if your self-image denotes that you are an entertaining public speaker, you will feel confident if called upon to speak in public and in all probability will perform very well. However, if your self-image denotes that you are introverted and retiring, the idea of public speaking will make you very nervous and hence your performance is likely to be poor. Our self-image has a massive effect upon the way we live our day-to-day lives.

Our self-image plays a key part in determining the amount of mental resistance we experience in any given situation. If our self-image states that we are easily up to a certain task, the mental resistance experienced will be minimal or even non-existent. However, if our self-image states that a certain task is way beyond our current capabilities, the mental resistance we experience will be great.

We tend to act in accordance with our self-image. It therefore has a huge effect upon our performance. Always remember that our self-image is a kind of master plan for how we live our lives. It should therefore be apparent that improving our self-image is a key part of enhancing our mental strength, overcoming mental resistance, and making progress towards our goals. So how do we improve our self-image? And, more importantly, where does our self-image come from?

Our self-image is constructed from our thoughts, our beliefs about ourselves and our experiences. To give an example, my self-image tells me that I'm an able martial artist. This belief stems from positive things that my coaches, my peers and my students have told me. It stems from all the positive experiences I've had, the competitions I've won, the gradings I've passed, the successful fights I've had etc. All the positive experiences I've had in the martial arts lead me to conclude that I'm an able martial artist. Therefore, I have the self-image of an able martial artist and act in accordance with that image. This self-image ensures that I act in a positive and confident way towards the martial arts. This helps me overcome the mental resistance I experience as I move into my zone of development and further develop my skills. By overcoming the mental resistance and moving into the zone of development, I increase my mental strength, gain more experience and have the opportunity to further develop my talent. These positive changes will further improve my self-image in relation to the martial arts. Positive experiences lead to a positive self-image. A positive self-image can lead to more positive experiences. However, it can also work the other way around.

When I was around twelve years old, the school I attended was putting on a show and every pupil was required to sing in it. There were a few solo pieces and every pupil had to sing a few lines in front of the remainder of the class in order to see if they were able to take on one of those solo roles. With a name like Abernethy I'm frequently at the top of any alphabetical list and hence I was required to go first. My singing was so bad that the teacher thought I was either feeling the pressure of going first, or that I was deliberately making a mess of it! I was informed to take it seriously and that I could do it again after everyone else. All the other pupils took their turn and again I was asked to sing. Again I was awful! I can't remember singing publicly prior to this event and therefore I had no real concept of the level of my ability. This experience informed me that I was a very poor singer and it formed that aspect of my self-image. If I did decide that I wanted to be a singer, then I would need to alter this self-image to make progress.

I'm sure you can think of many such events in your own life that have shaped your self-image. Whilst there are other influences on our self-image, experience is probably the most potent. We need to ensure we have positive experiences in relation to the areas in which we wish to progress and excel. As we'll see later on in this chapter, there are ways in which we can learn to reprogram our self-image and ensure that our thoughts are positive and strengthening. However, above all we need to ensure that we put our positive thoughts into action and therefore have positive experiences that fortify our strong self-image. We'll cover the importance of action in the following chapter.

There are a few important things we need to re-emphasise and explain at this point. The first and most important thing is that to make anything happen we need to act. If there is no action then there is no progress. Secondly, we need positive experiences not only to move us closer to our goals, but also to enhance our self-image and ensure that our mindset and our thoughts are able to help us progress yet further. Finally, we need to understand that a positive experience is not always a successful experience.

As a child, I certainly didn't win the first few martial arts tournaments I entered. In fact, I did very poorly! However, entering those tournaments was a positive experience even though I was unsuccessful. Initially I was very nervous, just entering the events had taken courage on my part. Hence, my self-image had been adjusted to include the aspect that I was now brave enough to enter tournaments. My self-image was also enhanced because I now had experience of martial arts tournaments. The experience wasn't successful if winning the tournament was the criteria for success. However, it was still a very positive experience as it had a positive effect upon my self-image and positioned me to make further progress in the martial arts.

The way we view an experience has a great deal to do with how our self-image responds to it and the effect that experience will have. Let's say that I had taken a negative view of my early tournaments and had viewed my failure to win as proof that I was no good at the martial arts. Then the same physical experience that had previously enhanced my self-image would have had a negative effect upon it.

We need to ensure that we always think positively. By keeping a positive outlook, and seeking the beneficial aspects of a situation, we ensure that we have many more opportunities to make progress and enhance our self-image. Being a success in any field has little to do with striving to win all the time, and then beating ourselves up if we don't. Being a success is more about making a consistent and concerted effort to encourage steady growth. We should concentrate on the process, rather than fixate on the product, if we wish to become a true success. With this outlook, we naturally find many more experiences to be positive in nature and therefore we grow much faster.

We can see how positive experiences can improve our self-image and therefore ensure we think and act in a positive and productive way, but what about the effect of negative experiences? How do we deal with negative experiences that have the potential to harm our self-image and erode our confidence?

The first and most important thing to remember is that we, and we alone, are in complete control of how we respond to any event. Even if a particular experience appears to have been a complete disaster, we can still transform it into a positive experience if we maintain a positive frame of mind. As an example, let's say an aspiring stand-up comedian gets booed off stage. If they have a negative mindset, the situation will erode their self-image and they may no longer see themselves as being funny or entertaining. Because our self-image forms a master plan to which we operate, it will be a major problem for a comedian if they operate to a plan which states that they are not funny!

If the comedian has a positive outlook, they see the situation as a great learning opportunity. They know for a fact that their material, and their delivery of that material, needs work. They can learn from the experience and get funnier. There can be very few comedy greats who didn't get booed off stage at sometime or other! If our comedian doesn't let the experience hold them back, then it proves they have the same staying power that all the greats have. This seemingly negative experience can improve self-image if the comedian has a positive outlook. The comedian now knows that they have staying power (they did not quit) and has a better understanding of how to be funny and entertaining (they know what does not work).

It is my belief that one of the most important attributes for success is tenacity. If you simply refuse to quit and never give up on your goals, it's hard to see how you can be anything other than a success. What others may see as failure, the mentally strong will see as a positive opportunity to foster tenacity, learn from experience and increase mental strength.

Experience is not the only thing that shapes our self-image. Our influences can also have a great effect. Your family, your friends, your school, your spouse, your environment etc. can all have a profound effect on your self-image. I once knew a gentleman whose father was always very critical of everything he did. Unsurprisingly, despite being a lovely guy and very talented, he lacked self-confidence. Although he had no real reason to, he got very nervous around people and doubted his own abilities. His father had created the negative self-image to which he operated. This false self-image had held him back and last time we spoke he was working to reprogram his self-image so that it reflects the person he really is.

All of us are affected by our influences. It is therefore important to ensure that we deal with any influence that affects our self-image in a negative way. If our self-image is negative, we will act in a negative way and never realise our full potential. In more severe cases this reassessment and reprogramming of our self-image may involve working with mental health professionals. It can be easy to see how things like a traumatic event or highly-critical parents can have a strong effect on our self-image. However, there are millions of other more minor influences that can also have a significant effect on the way we see ourselves and hence the thoughts we think.

Just as we need to be careful about what we take into our bodies if we are to be physically healthy, we need to be equally careful about what we take into our minds if we are to be mentally healthy. We must never allow negative thoughts to take root. As we discussed earlier in this book, when we are about to move outside our comfort zone, the presence of negative thoughts is a good indication we are about to make progress and expand our capabilities. However, we should never let negative thoughts get a grip inside our minds. If a negative thought is permitted to take root, it can become part of our self-image and we will then act in accordance with that image.

When negative thoughts appear, how should we deal with them? The first, and in many ways the most important thing to remember is that negative thoughts are generally at their strongest when you are about to break the bonds of your comfort zone and make meaningful progress towards your goal. This is the subconscious's attempt to talk you out of a situation it incorrectly perceives as a genuine threat. Negative thoughts are the weak and fearful aspects of our character. Because they are weak and fearful, they are never given much credibility by the mentally strong.

You must acknowledge that the presence of negative thoughts is a sure sign that you are about to move outside your comfort zone, become stronger, and progress towards your goal. It's a good thing those thoughts are there, as long as you don't let them take root in your mind. If you ignore their negative message and act in a positive way, not only will you develop your mental strength, but your positive action will shine a strong light on these shadowy saboteurs and they will promptly vanish.

There are times where the negative thought is strong enough to keep us frozen to the spot and hence no positive action is forthcoming. In these cases we have a number of differing options in order to ensure that progress is made. Firstly, it may be that you're not yet ready or mentally strong enough to make that particular move. In essence, the task is outside your zone of development. Simply take things a little slower, or reduce the target a little, so that you feel capable of attempting the reduced task. You'll always experience fear, negative thoughts, mental resistance etc. whenever you're making progress. You'll never be able to get rid of them completely, but by readjusting the length of your next step, you can keep them to a manageable level. Having taken the smaller step, you will have become mentally stronger and grow in confidence, and therefore become more able to accomplish the original target.

Another way to reduce paralysing negative thoughts is to replace them with positive thoughts. Sometimes it's not that we are incapable of accomplishing a certain task; it's just that we believe we are! If we can reprogram our self-image to believe we are capable of a task, we reduce the potency of the negative thoughts and the strength of the mental resistance. Remember, we are what we think. We operate to the master plan of our self-image. If we think we're capable of a certain task, we'll act like we are, we'll feel like we are, and in all probability we will indeed be capable of that task! One way to accomplish this reprogramming of our self-image is through positive affirmation.

Positive affirmation is simply the mental repetition of a positive statement. We repeatedly expose ourselves to a positive thought so that it takes root and forms part of our self-image. Let's say that you're nervous about a job interview and your mind is throwing up all kinds of negative thoughts. At regular intervals throughout your day, and every time a negative thought surfaces, you should mentally recite your positive affirmation. In the case of the job interview, it could be something along the lines of 'I have all the skills that this job requires and my talents always shine forth in interviews. I know I'm perfect for the job and so does everyone who interviews me.' Repeated exposure to these positive thoughts will counter your negative thinking and reprogram your self-image. The master plan will state that the interview will go well and hence you'll act in a positive and confident manner during the interview.

Negative thoughts encourage weakness. They are therefore weak in nature. In the presence of strong positive thoughts, the weak negative thoughts are overpowered and will disappear. However, there is an art to ensuring your thoughts are truly strong and truly positive. If you're not careful, what may at first appear to be a positive affirmation, can in fact have a negative effect. Your positive affirmations must have no trace of negativity.

One way in which negativity can creep into seemingly positive thoughts is through the incorrect use of tense. For example, let's say that you wanted to become a professional painter and have made moves in that direction. As a natural part of any progress, negative thoughts start to appear that cause you to doubt your talent. In order to counter these negative thoughts you use the affirmation of 'I will have the talent to be a highly successful professional painter.' Have you spotted the negativity in this seemingly positive statement? Because you've used the phrase 'I will have' it infers that you don't have the talent at this point in time.

In some ways the brain is like a computer: if you put faulty commands in, you get a faulty result out. Because the affirmation is faulty, your self-image will be one of someone who is striving for talent, but crucially does not have it at the moment. We always operate to the master plan and hence your positive affirmation is causing you to think and act like someone with insufficient talent! This seemingly positive affirmation will actually increase the potency of your negative thoughts! By removing the word 'will' so that the affirmation becomes 'I have the talent to be a highly successful professional painter', the affirmation will then have a strong positive effect.

Another way in which seemingly positive thoughts can have a negative effect is the inadvertent inclusion of a negative statement. To return to the example of a job interview, let's say that in order to counter your increasing nervousness, you mentally recited the affirmation of 'I will not be nervous in the interview.' The trouble with this seemingly positive statement is that it includes the words 'be nervous in the interview'! There is a negative statement tagging along for the ride! Every time we repeat that affirmation there is the strong possibility that our brains will pick up on the negative side of the statement by overlooking or ignoring the first three words. It could easily be that your self-image will be reprogrammed in such a way that your nervousness will actually increase! All positive affirmations should be 100 percent positive. In this situation an infinitely better affirmation would be 'I am relaxed and confident in interviews. I always perform well.'

When you mentally recite your affirmations you become a strong influence on yourself. You can reprogram, reshape and reform your self-image to ensure you think, feel and act in the strongest and most productive way. We are what we think. If we think strong thoughts, we are strong!

Another way to enhance our self-image and counter negative thoughts is through positive visualisation. If we can see ourselves being successful in our mind's eye, our subconscious counts this as a positive experience and hence adjusts our self-image accordingly. This may sound a little strange to some, but positive visualisation is a scientifically proven tool that is much used in elite level sport. Additionally, virtually every successful person I've ever met, regardless of their chosen field of excellence, makes use of this tool to some degree. Numerous scientific studies have shown that positive visualisation can have a marked effect on self-image and performance. One study even confirmed that just through visualising going for a run, we will actually become fitter!

The fundamental reason that visualisation works is that our subconscious is very poor at determining what's real and what isn't. As an example, if you watch a frightening or suspenseful film, it is highly likely that you'll experience the sensation of fear. The image on the cinema screen is not real and can't actually harm you, but your subconscious acts as if the image was real. Likewise, if we can project positive images into our mind's eye, the subconscious believes the visualised success to be real and therefore adjusts your self-image accordingly. But this can work both ways! If we inadvertently visualise negative things, which many people do by default, it will have a negative effect upon us. It is therefore very important to keep the images in our mind positive. Having the self-discipline to engage in positive visualisation on a regular basis will help us to maintain a positive mindset.

Positive visualisation simply involves relaxing and then seeing yourself being successful in whatever task it is that you want to excel at. My favoured method has always been to lie down and ensure I'm as comfortable as possible. I then take in a deep breath through my nose, hold it for a couple of seconds, and then exhale through my mouth. I try to concentrate solely on my breathing and will repeat the breathing cycle until I feel very relaxed. I then see myself being successful in as much detail as I can.

Sports psychologists have stated that, in order to make our visualisation as productive as possible, we need to make use of at least three of our five senses. In our visualisation we need to be aware of the sights, the sounds, the smells, the tactile sensations and even the taste of the successful environment and situation we see in our mind's eye. The more detail we can visualise, the more effective the visualisation will be in reshaping and enhancing our self-image. See yourself being a success at every stage of the activity. See yourself acting in a confident and positive way. Above all else, visualise with great intensity how great your success feels! Upon completion of the visualisation, relax for a little while longer and then just get on with the rest of your day.

As with positive affirmation, we need to ensure that negativity does not creep in during visualisation. Sometimes this attempted hijacking by negativity can be as unsubtle as your thoughts straying so that you actually visualise a negative outcome! It can also be a kind of negative soundtrack playing in the background so that although you're visualising a positive outcome, the background thoughts are along the lines of: 'It won't really happen that way! You're wasting your time with all the positive thinking, it won't work and everything is still certain to go wrong!' In these cases it's relatively easy to spot that things have gone astray. Upon realising this, we should draw ourselves back to a wholly positive visualisation.

Sometimes the negativity in our visualisation can be very subtle. It may be that you'll inadvertently visualise yourself as being smaller than you are, or that your mental image of yourself is less colourful (as in greyer) than the surrounding people and places. These types of subtle shift are indicative of negative thoughts being subtly present. You should be the most colourful, largest and radiant image around which everything else pales by comparison! All aspects of the visualisation need to be positive if you are to get the most benefit from your visualisation practise.

In my martial arts training I have used positive visualisation for over eighteen years. I can confirm through my own personal experience that visualisation works amazingly well. All the fights I have won, gradings I have passed, books I have written, and techniques I have applied have all been seen in my mind's eye before they became an actuality. I had successfully fought, successfully taken my grading exam, and successfully authored my books in my mind long before I'd physically done so. Therefore, my self-image was of someone who was a successful martial artist and author prior to attempting the tasks themselves! Because I'd formed a positive self-image, the master plan to which I operated was therefore one of success. As a result the mental resistance was overcome and my actions were positive. And the positive actions ensured that the positive visualisation became reality!

The human mind is the most complex thing in the known universe. Its power is vast. Almost everything you see around you once started as a thought inside someone's head. The book you're holding was once just a thought; the keyboard I'm typing on was once just a thought; the house you live in was once just a thought; the car you drive was once just a thought etc. I know it may sound a tad mystical, but the fact that our lives are shaped by our thoughts is profoundly down-to-earth. Our lives are shaped by our actions and our actions result from our thoughts. What we think about will manifest itself in our lives through the simple process of cause and effect. You are what you think. If you want a better and happier life, think better and happier thoughts!

You may come across some people who feel that by thinking in a positive way you are somehow being boastful or arrogant. In Chapter Twelve we'll discuss in detail how social conditioning and peer pressure sometimes encourages us to think negatively. For now it is enough to state that there is nothing wrong with thinking about yourself in a positive way and therefore fulfilling your potential.

Most people would agree that it's wrong to say negative things about others. Yet it is somehow socially acceptable to say negative things about ourselves! Indeed, when we think positively, it is often felt that we are being unrealistic, we are daydreaming, we are setting ourselves up for a fall or being arrogant. However, if we think in a negative way then we are often applauded for having our feet on the ground, for being realistic, practical and down-to-earth.

All this may lead us to wonder why the majority consider thinking negatively to be realistic whilst thinking positively is considered unrealistic. The reason is simply because the majority of people think negatively; therefore they have a negative or, at best, a compromised self-image. They act in accordance with their self-image and therefore their negative thoughts become a reality. This leads many to conclude that thinking negatively is therefore realistic, which it is for all those who think negatively! However, for those who think positively, your positive thoughts are also realistic. Never be afraid to think big!

In this chapter we have seen how we are what we think and how we can make ourselves stronger through thinking positive thoughts and adjusting our self-image. That is not to say that thinking positively is easy; it isn't! To overcome all the negative conditioning you may have received, you need to make a concerted effort to think positively all the time. Your positive thinking needs to become habitual. Whenever a negative thought starts to take hold, realise it is a kind of mental poison that must be attacked with the vigour and contempt it deserves. Have the mental strength to banish negativity from your mind and replace it with strong, powerful and positive thoughts. We are what we think. If we think strong thoughts we become strong.

By thinking the right thoughts we can change the way we view ourselves and hence become stronger and more able to accomplish the goals we have set for ourselves. Thinking the right thoughts is a prerequisite of success. In order to live great lives, we need to consistently think great thoughts!

Chapter 7

The Importance of Action

'Many a false step is made by standing still'
– Unknown

Action is the fundamental cause of success. However, we can occasionally find ourselves turning a blind eye to this obvious truth. For anything to happen there needs to be some form of action. Nothing can be achieved if we remain static.

In order to develop mental strength we need to act. We need to face up to mental resistance, leave the comfort zone and move into our zone of development. If we wish to make progress and achieve our goals, staying still is not an option. There is never a good reason for procrastination. Planning, pondering, visualising, wishing and dreaming don't mean anything without action.

It is vital that you appreciate that action is always required before anything will alter or improve. If an activity scares you, the fear will always remain until you attempt that activity. There is no point in waiting for the fear to disappear, because it never will! Upon attempting that activity, you gain experience of that activity and hence are better able to cope with it in the future. Therefore, the fear associated with that activity will reduce. The more experience you have, the smaller the fear will be. If you don't act, the fear will always be present and you will find yourself imprisoned by it.

You may also believe that a certain activity is beyond you. Since I wrote my first book, I've had an innumerable amount of people tell me that they'd also like to write a book. When I tell them that they should, and it's really not that difficult if you're prepared to stick with it, I normally get a long list of reasons why they can't. Chief among these reasons is the belief that they have no talent for writing. The answer to this perceived problem is to develop their talent for writing, and the way to do that is to write! If you want to be a painter, then paint. If you want to travel the world, then travel. If you want to be a millionaire, start up a business. And if you want to be writer, then write.

I'm greatly amused by the term 'writer's block'. In case you've never come across this term before, writer's block is what writers call an apparent affliction (i.e. a profound lack of inspiration) that temporarily robs them of their ability to write. No other craft has the luxury of a block and I don't see why we writers should consider ourselves to be anything special! To illustrate how absurd this idea is, what would you think of a plumber who couldn't come and fix your leaky water pipes because they were suffering from plumber's block ?!? Sometimes my writing just flows out of me; other times I have to force it. Either way the important thing is that I write. Without the action of writing, I'm simply not a writer.

I'd challenge you to think of anything you value that didn't require some action to bring it into your life? I can't think of a single thing! You can wish and hope for things as much as you like; you'll never get them until you make a determined effort to get them.

As a martial arts instructor, I regularly get people telling me that they'd love to study the martial arts, but they wouldn't know what to do! Well, how will they ever know what to do if they never get started? This experience is common to almost every instructor I've ever talked to. This is very similar to the people, and there are a lot of them, who say they'd like to go to the gym but aren't fit enough! Isn't that why people go to the gym in the first place?

By giving reasons why they can't do something, people either have no real interest in the activity (but are saying they do out of politeness), they are adopting the victim mentality in order to avoid leaving the comfort zone, or they don't understand the importance of action. To progress towards any goal, you need to act. You need to take the first step. If you want to write that book, then start writing. If you want to get fitter, start exercising. If you want that dream job, start making calls and sending off that CV. Action always comes first! Mental strength, self-belief, talent and confidence all come later. It's impossible to grow in any way without first gaining experience of the activity. And the only way to get experience is through action.

The amount of effort we can put into procrastination would be better spent on advancing us towards our goals. Underlying any procrastination is the desire to stay in the comfort zone for as long as possible. To make any progress, we need to act, and we need to act now! Delay can be dangerous.

By delaying our positive action we give mental resistance more time to grow and we give negative thoughts more time to rattle around in our heads. We will come up with more and more reasons not to move forward. We will then start to accept those reasons and what started off as a temporary delay becomes permanent. Indeed, this is one of the primary tactics that our outdated survival mechanism uses to induce inactivity. If we really want to move forward, the negative, fearful part of our mind may try to convince us that one day we really will act, but not just yet.

Throughout my time in the martial arts, I've regularly found myself in unnerving situations. What I've found is that inactivity makes fear grow stronger. As an example, let's say that I'm about to have a heavy spar with a more able and larger opponent. If I procrastinate and try to put off that fight by sparring with other people first (like I did in my early days in the martial arts) my fear of that big fight will grow. It's almost as if your subconscious observes your fearful actions and then uses them as justification to increase those fear levels.

I've found that the best way to get rid of fear is to face the situation head on. If I decide to spar with the person I'm scared of first, the negative, whinging part of my brain is made to shut up! It can't keep telling me I'm scared because my actions demonstrate I'm not. I also begin to feel proud of myself for not letting my fear dictate and control my actions. By facing up to that fear, it begins to subside.

Fear, doubt and negativity get more intense the longer you put off the activity. By waiting for them to subside before acting, you may very well intensify those feelings. It is only through flexing our mental strength and making ourselves act that those negative feelings will begin to subside. We need to take that first step positively and with conviction.

In many ways, the first step is the most important. We tend to forget that those we admire once made that exact same step. The martial artists that I really look up to were all beginners once. There was a time when the world's best writers had written nothing. All the great painters had to paint their first picture. In fact, all the greats in any field had to take a first step at some point. They, just like us, had to overcome those fears and doubts and take their initial action. Whilst some wish for things to get easier (which won't happen) before acting, the successful get out there and get going. The unfulfilled masses wish that one day they'll get their way; the successful go out and make their way.

Despite all the perceived difficulties that stand in your way, you need to act. And the time for that action is NOW! Not only do things get harder the longer you leave them, but you're running out of time! I hate to be the one to break it to you, but the cold, hard fact is that you're now closer to death than you were when you started reading this page.

Death is frequently regarded as a morbid subject and is therefore something that most people prefer not to think or talk about. We try to turn a blind eye to the fact that one day we'll all stop breathing, and by default we live our lives like we have an eternity to do all the things we'd like to. We don't.

Many years ago I was out walking my dog on a route that takes me close to the local cemetery. It was a cold, crisp winter's night and I decided I'd pop into the cemetery to visit the grave of a friend who'd been killed in an accident. I knelt at the grave and read all the cards and messages by the moonlight. As I did so, I thought about how tragic his death was. He was a very nice guy and very talented. I couldn't help thinking about what he could have achieved if he'd just had more time.

I left the grave of my friend and continued on my walk. A few minutes later, with the thoughts of my friend still in my mind, I stopped and looked up at the sky. The sky was very clear and as I stared towards the heavens I was in awe at the number of stars I could see. I thought about how the light from each one of those stars took hundreds of years to get here and about how large and timeless the universe was.

The combined thoughts of the vastness of the universe and the tragic shortness of my friend's life converged in my mind and caused a sudden, powerful fear to surge though my body. For the first time in my life I was acutely aware that my time on this planet was running out. With every frosty breath I was closer to the time that I would die! This was not the intellectual understanding of the limits of life that we all have, but the hard-hitting emotional reality of that fact. I knew I was running out of one-days (we all are) and that I needed to start pursuing my dreams whilst there was time left to do so.

I've never experienced the reality of death as acutely as I did that day. Although, at the times where I know I'm not giving as much as I could, I wish I could feel those sensations again in order to refocus my mind.

We don't have an eternity to do the things we want to do and to achieve all the things we want to achieve. All we have is the here and now. You can achieve anything you want. But you need to act and act now!

Chapter 8

Developing Talent

'Adversity has the effect of eliciting talents,
which would otherwise have lain dormant'
– Horace

In addition to having the mental strength to achieve our goals, we also need the talent. To be a world-class footballer, you not only need the mental strength to succeed, you also need the talent to play at world-level. Contrary to much prevailing thought, talent is not something you either have or you don't. Talent can be developed and we'll look at how that process works in this chapter.

As we progress towards our goals, mental resistance is not the only type of resistance we will experience. In addition to the resistance that exists within our minds, we will also experience resistance in the form of changes and obstacles in the outside world. We will refer to these outside challenges as external resistance.

We will only ever experience external resistance if we lack, or think we lack, the talent needed to accomplish a given task. If we have the talent, we will accomplish the required task with ease. There will be no external resistance. Just as our mental strength enables us to overcome mental resistance, it is our skills and talents that allow us to overcome external resistance. However, as we shall see, mental strength and talent are closely linked and have a strong effect upon one another.

In previous chapters we discussed how moving outside the comfort zone in order to attempt a challenging task (an external resistance) can result in negative thoughts and feelings (mental resistance). However, as we'll see later on in this chapter, the process also works the other way around with mental resistance making the challenges and external resistances we face harder to overcome.

Negative and discouraging thoughts are likely to appear every time we attempt to advance towards our goals. These discouraging thoughts form a mental resistance that we need to overcome if we are to achieve the things we want in life. Now here's the good bit: by utilising our mental strength to overcome mental resistance, we can also develop the talent needed to overcome external resistance!

Mental resistance is only ever experienced when you are about to move outside your current comfort zone. If you're totally comfortable with the task you're about to undertake, your survival instinct won't consider it any kind of threat and therefore it won't try to dissuade you from undertaking that task. However, if mental resistance is present it means that our survival instinct believes (rightly or wrongly) that we lack the talent to effectively undertake the task.

If we can push beyond that initial mental resistance and undertake the task, we may be pleasantly surprised to find that we do have sufficient talent (nice when that happens!). On the other hand, we may also find that the task was beyond our current capabilities. But we won't know until we try!

Unless we undertake the task, we'll never know if we're up to it or not. If we are, then great. And if it proves to be a struggle, then even better! Like the weightlifter who easily lifts a weight, on the one hand he's had a success. On the other hand there was not a sufficient resistance for them to benefit from that lift. If we attempt a task and struggle, we have the opportunity to grow. If we succeed with ease, nice though that is, we won't be able to grow from that experience. Developing talent works in a similar way. We'll discuss the exact mechanism in a moment. For now it is enough to understand that we need to be struggling in order to grow our talent.

An analogy may make things a little clearer. Let's say that we have a boxer who wants to be world champion. He regularly spars with everyone in his gym and defeats them all with ease. He knows that he's much better than his sparring partners and therefore experiences no mental resistance prior to sparring. Because our boxer is clearly the top dog in this environment, and therefore he never struggles when he spars, he will not be able to develop his talent to a world-class standard as long he remains in that environment. Knowing this, our boxer decides to seek out better quality sparring partners.

The first time our boxer spars with his new partners, he will experience mental resistance. He will experience negative and discouraging thoughts, and he will have to overcome these thoughts if he is to actually get in the ring and spar. The boxer understands mental resistance and takes its presence as a sign that he's taking a step in the right direction towards his goals. He utilises his mental strength, overcomes the mental resistance, and gets in the ring to spar.

Once in the ring, one of two things can happen. The boxer may find that the new partner, although better than his previous partners, still poses no real threat and he defeats them with ease. It will undoubtedly feel nice to learn that he's better than he thought, but the easy victory won't do anything to increase his talent or move him towards his world-title. Although this may seem like a bit of a paradox, the boxer would be better, from the perspective of developing his talent, if he lost!

If it transpires that the new sparring partner is much better than the boxer, he has the opportunity to develop his talent. Through sparring with people who are better than he is, and therefore struggling, the boxer will become acutely aware of all the faults and errors in his game. Previously, due to the relatively poor quality of his sparring partners, he could make all kinds of mistakes and still win with ease. Because of this, he is unlikely to be made aware of his errors. The new, more skilful sparring partner will be able to exploit the chinks in the armour and because the boxer is now aware of his failings, he can work to correct them and hence grow his talent.

From this example, we can see that through overcoming mental resistance, the boxer was able to move outside his current comfort zone and gain experience of sparring with better quality boxers. Through the experience gained, the boxer will become more aware of his strengths and shortfalls. He can then set about correcting those faults and building on his strengths in order to further develop his talent. Experience is a good teacher! And the only way to gain experience is to have the mental strength to overcome mental resistance and step outside your comfort zone.

When we move outside the comfort zone to undertake challenging new tasks, we gain the opportunity to test our skills, learn from the experience and then grow our talent. However, we need to attempt the task in a positive way if we are to benefit from the experience. To better illustrate the need to face challenges in a positive way, I'd like to return to the analogy of the boxer who has decided to train with better quality sparring partners.

Let's say that the boxer has overcome enough mental resistance to get in the ring, but some of the negative thoughts that made up that mental resistance still remain. He doubts his ability to hold his own at this new level. He is listening to the negative thoughts, and he is therefore very unlikely to give a positive performance.

The boxer is having recurring thoughts along the lines of 'I'm going to get badly beaten!' The fact that the thoughts initially surfaced is a good indicator that the boxer is engaging in an activity that will advance him along his chosen path. So in that regard, it's a good thing they are there. However, if the boxer does not use his mental strength to overcome those thoughts he will then start to believe that he truly is going to get badly beaten! This belief will obviously affect the boxer's self-image, and hence he will fight like he's about to get beaten! He is very unlikely to fight in a positive way and his negative thoughts will become a self-fulfilling prophecy.

As we said before, through struggling, the boxer will gain the opportunity to learn from experience and therefore grow his talent. However, not on this occasion! Because the boxer did not fight to the best of his ability, it was not a true test of his talent. If he had fought in a positive way, it could have been a much closer fight. However, because the boxer did not fight to his limits, many lessons that could have been learnt have been lost. The main lesson the boxer can take away from this fight is the need to not undermine himself! The mental resistance caused the boxer to fight poorly. On this occasion, the mental resistance increased the external resistance (robbed the boxer of his true talent).

Like our boxer, you need to ensure that you face your challenges in a positive way if you are to gain the opportunity to learn from those experiences and therefore grow your talent. Negative thoughts will be present when you first commit to attempting a challenging task. The initial presence of these negative thoughts is a sure sign that you're moving in a positive direction. However, to make that step effective and meaningful, you need to ensure that you don't take those negative thoughts as the gospel truth. If you do, you will self-sabotage your advancement. In Chapter Six we looked at how we can counter negative thoughts and replace them with positive ones. In order to improve ourselves with the greatest efficiency, it's important to utilise the information covered in Chapter Six so that you prevent negative thoughts from having a negative effect on your performance.

The boxer from our example should have acknowledged the negative thoughts for what they are. Negative thoughts are a sign that you're doing positive things to advance towards your goal. They also provide an opportunity to develop our mental strength. They are not the tellers of truth! He should have acknowledged the messenger, but ignored the message. The boxer should have mentally countered his negative thoughts: 'The fact that I initially thought I'm not up to this is a sure sign that I'm progressing towards that world title! I'm proud of myself for having the courage and drive to advance myself and my skills. I'm strong enough and talented enough to spar at this level. It's what I need to do to progress. I'm up to this!' The negative message is effectively shouted down and the boxer is much more likely to give a true account of his abilities.

Just having the minimal amount of mental strength to attempt an activity is not enough if we wish to truly advance. We must always attempt any activity in a positive way that utilises all of our talent. If you give it your all and succeed, that's great! You've a good success under your belt and you'll be one step closer to your goal. If you give it your all and don't succeed, that's also great! You've gained experience, learnt some valuable lessons, and are now in a position to grow your talent. If you don't give it your all and fail, then you've wasted an opportunity. If you don't give it your all and succeed, then it's a sure sign that the activity undertaken was far too easy and no worthwhile progress has been made.

I feel it's worth mentioning here that worthwhile failure (giving it your all and still not accomplishing your immediate goal) is often a meaningful part of progress. If you never fail, then it is possible that you're constantly aiming too low and are never truly expanding your boundaries. As a martial artist for most of my life, I know that if I'm constantly winning my sparring matches, my skills are not being advanced. The failure from which we can learn, and therefore increase our talent, is a positive part of the process. The only true failure is the pointless failure from which no lessons can be learnt and no progress made.

We must understand that true success is not about succeeding with ease the first time we try. It's about perseverance, following the process, and developing our strength and talent as we go.

In order to learn from our experiences, so that we may develop our talents, we need to be honest with ourselves about our performance, our strengths and our shortfalls. It is only through an honest appraisal of our abilities that we can then set about improving those abilities. However, if we are not careful, we may be either too harsh or too lenient with ourselves.

When we are too harsh with ourselves it is normally because we have listened to the voice of mental resistance, taken onboard some of what it has said, and then used the perceived failure to justify the statements of that mental resistance.

Whenever you're about to attempt a challenging task, you are sure to have negative thoughts. When those negative thoughts surface, you should acknowledge that mental resistance is present, which means you're on the path to achieving your goals! You should then totally ignore what those negative thoughts are telling you. Remember that the job of mental resistance is to talk you out of activities your survival mechanism considers risky (and it's too outdated to give an objective assessment!). It will spout any old rubbish to convince you to play it safe. Don't believe something which you know has a hidden agenda, which you know is often scared of things it has no real reason to be, and which you know will lie to achieve its aims; even if that something is part of you!

You should shout down and drown out all negative thoughts with positive counter-thoughts. However, let's say that you didn't remove all the negative thoughts. You may still attempt that task, but at the back of your mind there may be a part of you that is expecting things to go badly! Not only will this make it more likely that things will go badly, it can also prevent you from learning from the experience in an objective way.

Upon attempting the task, some things may have gone well. Other things not so well. If you analysed the outcome in an objective way, you may be able to learn some lessons. However, if you've listened to the message of mental resistance, it can take root. Instead of looking at the outcome in a balanced way, you are likely to be too harsh on yourself and focus on the negative i.e. you knew things were going to go badly and now you have proof! You may conclude that the positive things were down to luck, and that the negative things are the symptoms of a catastrophic lack of talent. If you are overly harsh with yourself, an opportunity to grow talent has been lost. In order to grow our talent, we need to look at our performance objectively.

As well as being overly harsh when looking at how we can learn from the outcome of any given task, we can also be too lenient on ourselves. Attempting a challenging task will point out areas where our talent is lacking. However, we may sometimes be tempted to turn a blind eye to our shortcomings.

Whenever we attempt a task we gain the opportunity to learn from experience and increase our talent. However, if we don't accept that it is our responsibility to address any shortfalls, or if we don't accept that those shortfalls exist, we can't grow our talent and we can't progress. We should always be positive in our outlook, but we should avoid being 'positive' to the point where we can't see our shortcomings! We also have to accept that the level of our talent is our own responsibility. If we are not at the level that we want to be, then it's up to us to get there.

Thinking positively is very important. However, positive thinking is not the only thing required to succeed; we also need the talent. The only way we can grow our talent is through an honest appraisal of our strengths and weaknesses. Armed with that knowledge, we are then in a position to build upon our strengths and address our weaknesses in a positive and meaningful way.

Having a positive mindset does not mean ignoring any problems or deluding ourselves. Being positive is acknowledging any problems in an objective way and then taking positive steps to address those problems. If you find your talent lacking, take positive steps to learn from the experience and therefore increase your talent. This way you will advance and your talent will not be found wanting on future occasions.

When we are attempting to learn from an experience, it is very important to remain disciplined and not succumb to the temptations of overly harsh self-critique or the false elation of shortfall blindness.

In addition to your own assessment of your strengths and weaknesses, it is also possible to make use of the critiques of others in order to grow your talent. As with your own analysis of your performance, there are also opportunities and dangers when analysing the opinions of others. We'll discuss how we can make objective use of the views of others in Chapter Eleven.

So far in this chapter we've discussed how mental strength helps us to overcome mental resistance and therefore gain experience. If we approach all tasks in a positive way, and are objective about the outcome, we are then able to learn from experience and increase our talent. As our talents grow, we will be able to face up to increasingly greater external resistances and get ever closer to our goals.

We can only grow our talent through leaving the comfort zone. It is very common for people to use a perceived lack of talent to justify remaining within the comfort zone. How many times have you heard someone say that they'd love to be able to do something but they lack the talent? You must leave the comfort zone to develop talent rather than waiting for the talent to magically appear! Flex your mental strength, overcome mental resistance, leave the comfort zone, learn from experience, and a growth in talent becomes inevitable.

One form of mental resistance that you are very likely to experience when you're about to leave the comfort zone is the fear of making a complete mess of any impending task. My grandfather is a very skilled carpenter. He's well into his eighties now and rarely practises his craft, but in his working years he was well-known in our community for the skill of his work. When talking about carpentry, my grandfather said, 'When making anything, the first thing you need to make is a mess!' He was referring to the inevitable scattering of sawdust, off-cuts, tools etc. that occurs when a job begins. However, I think there is a wider message within that statement. Whenever we attempt to make progress, we need to accept that one of the first things we're likely to make is a mess!

If we are attempting a task that is genuinely beyond our current skill level, we need to be comfortable with the fact that there is a possibility we'll make a complete mess of it! And that's OK because we'll analyse the outcome, learn from the experience, and grow our talent. However, it is possible that we can fear making a fool of ourselves so much that we may avoid undertaking the task altogether!

I'm going to let you in on a little secret; this chapter was a complete mess until it had been rewritten several times! On the first draft, I wrote my daily quota of words, came back to read over it the next day, and was utterly appalled by the gibberish that I'd written! And that's fine, because once I'd made the mess, I found myself in a better position to rewrite the parts of the chapter that didn't work.

I also made a mess the first time I taught a martial arts class. My teaching was unstructured and my communications skills were poor. I couldn't motivate people and I was unable to inspire self-discipline in the students. However through attempting to teach, and learning from experience, I was able to improve my teaching skills and I'm now in a position where I teach martial arts for a living.

For a number of years I was a national level judge in the martial arts (I've since stopped refereeing in order to devote more time to my writing etc.). The first time I did some judging, I was so bad they took me off the area! I'd made the mess and three years later I was a national level tatami chief.

Don't be afraid of making a mess of something. It's often a natural part of the process. Successful people don't just appear. They go though the same process we all do on our way to where we want to be. How many millionaires have had business deals go bad? How many professional entertainers were booed off stage at one point in their careers? How many inventors had prototypes fail in spectacular fashion? My guess would be most, if not all of them!

Never be afraid of making a mess of things or making a fool of yourself. There will always be people who lack the mental strength and courage to progress toward their own goals. Those same people often feel threatened when you make progress towards your goals. It reminds them that they could do the same if they had the mental strength to do so. They therefore feel vindicated in their inactivity when you stumble on your journey. It is also that kind of person who is normally quick to point the finger or revel in what they incorrectly perceive as your failure. Don't be afraid of making a mess of things. It's part of the process! Leave the comfort zone behind, gain experience, learn from that experience and grow your talents.

Learning from experience is not the only opportunity for developing talent that moving outside the comfort zone affords us. We will also begin to find ourselves around the right people. When I first started writing I didn't know any authors, editors, printers, publishers, designers or typesetters. As a consequence of leaving my comfort zone and attempting to get my work published, I came into contact with people working in the publishing industry. The help and assistance that these people provided helped me to grow my talent as a writer.

A similar thing happened with my martial arts training. As I developed as a martial artist, I found myself coming in to regular contact with an ever greater array of very talented people, all of whom were able to provide information, feedback, guidance and motivation. By gradually increasing my comfort zone, and by not being afraid to leave it, the range of people I have direct access to has grown ever larger. I now regularly train and converse with masters, world-renowned martial artists, international referees, world-level competitors, and incredibly skilled fighters from many different martial systems from all over the world. My skills as a martial artist are obviously enhanced by being in contact with such people.

We'll cover how other people can help us to increase our mental strength, progress towards our goals and develop our talent in more detail in Chapter Ten. For now it is enough to understand that having the mental strength to move outside your comfort zone will bring you into contact with people who will be able to help you grow your talent.

You can liken the comfort zone to goldfish in a bowl. Goldfish can only grow in proportion to the size of the bowl in which they are kept. If you keep goldfish in a small bowl, they can't grow. Likewise, if you don't expand your comfort zone, you can't grow. By constantly moving into the zone of development, it is an inevitable consequence that you'll become mentally stronger and more talented. You should always aim to be the small fish in the big pond. That way you know that you're growing.

To recap, when we attempt tasks and activities that we perceive as being beyond the capabilities of our talents, we gain the opportunity to grow those talents. Prior to attempting those tasks and activities, mental resistance will be present. Providing you have the mental strength to overcome that mental resistance, you will gain the opportunity to grow your talent!

Using your mental strength to overcome mental resistance will ensure that you gain experience, learning opportunities, and that you will come into contact with people who will be able to help you grow your talent. As your talent grows you will be able to overcome ever greater challenges and external resistances.

If you have the mental strength to get out into the big wide world and attempt to fulfil your dreams, the situations and the people you need to grow your talent will be naturally forthcoming. Follow the process and nothing will be able to hold you back!

Chapter 9

Proactive and Everyday Resistance

*'I am grateful for all my problems… as each of them was
overcome I became stronger and more able to meet
those yet to come. I grew in all my difficulties'*
– J.C. Penney

In the last chapter, we looked at mental and external resistance
and discussed how we can use both mental strength and
talent to overcome these resistances and progress towards our
goals. We can also subdivide all the resistance we will face in
life into two broad categories; proactive resistance and everyday
resistance.

Proactive resistance refers to the resistance that we actively
seek out in order to overcome that resistance, strengthen
ourselves mentally, develop our talents and make progress
towards our goals.

By contrast, everyday resistance is the difficulties and
problems that enter our everyday lives. We didn't proactively
seek out this resistance, but nevertheless it is present in our
life. All the resistance we experience, regardless of its origin,
has the potential to strengthen us when correctly approached.
We'll now move on to discuss both types of resistance in more
detail, starting with proactive resistance.

In physical training there is a principle known as the SAID
principle. The letters SAID stand for 'Specific Adaptation to
Imposed Demand'. What this means is that our bodies
specifically adapt to meet specific challenges.

Let's say that I wanted to improve my stamina for my martial arts sparring. I could go running. Running is a great form of exercise that has a very positive effect on cardiovascular fitness. If I run consistently, my body will adapt in accordance with the new demands placed upon it and I will become a better runner. Although running will have a positive effect on my cardiovascular fitness, I'm not really looking to become a better runner! I want to have more stamina when I spar. Therefore I need to spar for longer periods of time at a greater intensity. If I give myself the specific demand (I spar for longer periods of time at a greater intensity), I'll get the specific adaptation (my stamina for sparring will improve). By engaging in the specific activity, I will adapt specifically for that activity. Sparring harder and for longer will undoubtedly improve my stamina for sparring. However, it won't necessarily make me a better runner.

If you watch the Olympic Games, or any other similar event, you'll notice that long-distance runners look and perform very differently from sprinters. The reason for this is the SAID principle.

Long-distance runners train by running long distances. This causes the specific changes needed to enhance their ability to run long distances. Practising sprinting over one-hundred metres would do little to improve their ability to keep up a strong pace over twenty-six miles. Likewise, the sprinter will train by practising explosive bursts over a short distance. This won't enhance their endurance – which is OK because they don't need endurance for their chosen event – but it will cause their body to adapt in specific ways that will increase their ability to run very quickly over short distances.

In order to best develop our mental strength and talent, we need to engage in activities specifically related to our goals. This can be best achieved by setting specific goals (we'll look at goal setting later on in this book). For now, the key thing to appreciate is that the SAID principle applies to our mental development just as much as our physical development.

It is possible to be mentally strong in one area and weak in another (in a similar way to how an Olympic sprinter won't be a good marathon runner). To use myself as an example, as a result of teaching classes and seminars for many years, I'm very confident when it comes to public speaking. However, I'd be mentally weak if asked to sing in public. I have very little experience of singing, no talent for singing, and no confidence when it comes to singing. I'd therefore be very nervous, awkward and embarrassed if asked to sing in public. Thankfully, for me (and any potential listeners!), I have no interest in singing. But if I did, I'd need to impose the specific demand in order to get the specific adaptation, e.g. I'd need to practise singing in public in order to become better at it. My experience at talking in public has developed specific strengths and abilities, which may not overlap in to other areas (a specific adaptation to a specific imposed demand).

To ensure we develop ourselves in exactly the right way, we need to engage in activities specifically related to our goals in order to experience the specific, and therefore most beneficial, type of resistance. By engaging in the required activity, we will experience the exact mental resistance and obstacles required to increase our mental strength and develop our talent. By choosing to engage in activities related to our goals, and proactively taking steps to seek out proactive resistance, all the things we need to achieve our goals will naturally come our way.

To quickly recap, proactive resistance is the resistance we actively seek out in order to specifically develop our mental strength and talent. You can also think of proactive resistance as the beneficial resistance we actively bring into our lives through our own positive action. We'll now move on to explain everyday resistance in more depth.

Unlike proactive resistance, we don't actively seek out everyday resistance. Everyday resistance is the unforeseen problems and challenges that exist in our everyday lives. Everyday resistance is the everyday things that light our fuses, push our buttons or bring us down.

Whether we are striving for our goals or not, everyday resistance will undoubtedly come our way. Everyday resistance can be defined as 'the unwanted hassles and obstacles that can result in us reacting in a negative way.' The following are some examples of everyday resistance in effect:

Your alarm clock goes off when you've had a really bad night's sleep. You're instantly in a low way. You wish it was the weekend so you could stay in bed a bit longer.

You're late for an important meeting and you can't find your car keys. You lose your temper as a result.

A friend has a big success and you feel jealous.

You've just finished a long and really important piece of work when your computer crashes. Your blood boils and you start to spit profanities at the monitor.

You're trying to lose weight, but that bit of chocolate is just too irresistible. You eat it, and then instantly feel really guilty.

In all those examples, you're experiencing an everyday resistance that makes you react in a negative way. The alarm clock going off made you depressed. Your absent car keys made you lose your temper. Your friend's success made you jealous. The computer made you furious. The chocolate made you eat it and made you feel guilty. The fact is that none of these events made you do or feel anything. It is your reaction to that event that is the culprit!

When an event like those listed above occurs, we often feel the strong desire to act in a negative way or to feel negative emotions. But we don't have to behave in a negative way or experience negative emotions just because our subconscious prompts us to! We could flex our mental strength, overcome the everyday resistance, and then address the situation in a more positive way.

In physical training there is a method of training called cross-training. This means that in addition to engaging in your main activity, you also engage in related activities that will have a positive effect on the core skills you desire. For example, in addition to my martial arts training, I also lift weights to enhance my strength, and I run, cycle, row etc. in order to increase my endurance. At first glance this may seem contradictory to the SAID principle, but it isn't. The reason that the SAID principle is not being violated is that the vast majority of my training is martial arts based and the other activities are supplementary support activities. These support activities bring about adaptations that augment the main adaptations caused by my core training.

A person who does not practise martial arts will not develop any martial skills by running and lifting weights. However, a martial artist who runs and lifts weights will become a better martial artist due to the improvements in their physical condition. We must always ensure that we get plenty of experience of the main activity; however, cross-training will give a variety of activities that all have direct and indirect benefits to the main activity.

As we mentally develop ourselves, we can make use of everyday resistance as a form of mental cross-training to more broadly develop our overall mental strength and improve the quality of our day-to-day lives.

When we experience everyday resistance, we frequently get the strong urge to react. Now there can be no doubt that sometimes our strong response is justifiable and correct. For example, if you were to witness a loved one being attacked I'm sure you'd be filled with anger and the desire to act. Witnessing the event caused a reaction, but I'm sure we can all agree that the reaction is correct and healthy. However, there are many minor situations where giving in to the desire to react is not appropriate and can be counterproductive.

Is misplacing your keys really worth getting angry about? Will your anger do anything to help you find your keys? Will screaming at your crashed computer help you to fix it? It can certainly feel good to blow off a little steam, but then again your reaction may very well make the situation worse.

Many years ago, I had a computer crash on me immediately after I'd just completed a very laborious and difficult piece of work. Many things had gone wrong that day and that was the final straw! My response, I'm ashamed to admit, was to fling both arms up the air and shout profanities at the ceiling! As I threw my arms upward, I banged one of my knuckles on the desk (I later found out that I'd broken it). This further enraged me so I stood up and kicked my chair. The chair then flew across the room and hit the opposite wall. I didn't know it at the time, but a colleague of mine had come out of their office to find out what the shouting was all about and to see if they could be of help. As they did so, they were greeted by the sight of my chair hitting the wall! Unsurprisingly, they went back inside their office.

Did my anger make be feel better? Immediately, yes it did. But in the longer term, definitely not! It didn't bring my work back, it prevented my friend from helping me redo the work (although it did give them a good laugh!) and it caused me a lot of pain. The knuckle took months to get back to full strength and hurt like mad for weeks. My anger was counterproductive and on that occasion I failed to control it. Instead of taking control of the situation, the situation was controlling me. In mental strength terms, I'd failed to overcome the resistance.

It would have been more productive to flex my mental strength and overcome the everyday resistance. I should have taken a few deep breaths and calmed down. Perhaps I should have even seen the funny side of the situation. I'd have had no broken knuckle, no damaged chair and I'd have had help redoing the work.

When we feel ourselves controlled by a situation, we need to flex our mental strength so that we're back in charge of that situation. By not reacting in negative and unnecessary ways to day-to-day events, we develop a broad base of mental strength that will improve the quality of our lives and can help to develop the attributes that make us capable of achieving our goals.

With the correct approach, our day-to-day lives can be one long strengthening process. I'm sure you'll face situations that push your buttons at various points throughout almost every day. By overcoming the everyday resistance that comes our way, we will become mentally stronger. The mental strength, self-mastery and emotional control developed through the overcoming of everyday resistance will also help us to overcome the proactive resistance associated with achieving our goals.

The other major positive effect of overcoming everyday resistance is that you'll be better able to handle those same situations in the future. You'll expand your day-to-day comfort zone so that events that did stress or depress you now have no effect. Avoiding all that unnecessary stress will not only make your everyday existence more enjoyable, it will also conserve your energy for the things that really count.

It's important to understand that overcoming everyday resistance does not mean repressing or delaying your reaction. By way of example let's say that a colleague at work makes a statement that really angers you. Deciding that it's not appropriate to react, you recognise this as an opportunity for a bit of mental cross-training. You don't say anything to your colleague and on the surface you appear quite calm, but underneath you're seething with rage! If that anger remains there, sooner or later it will have to come out (normally in the direction of someone who has done nothing to deserve it!).

The everyday resistance was not overcome, nor were you in control of the situation. You still reacted; you just delayed that reaction to a later time.

If, when the anger started to appear, you'd decided that a few ill-chosen words really weren't worth getting riled about, and you'd had sufficient mental strength to cause the anger to disappear, then the everyday resistance would have been overcome. You would have been in complete control of yourself and the situation and your mental strength would have been developed. Should a similar event occur in the future, the anger is less likely to rise in the first place, which will make for a better day and will conserve your energy for your personal advancement. The mental strength developed will also help you to overcome the proactive resistance you'll experience on your way towards your goals.

Another aspect to everyday resistance is the desire to engage in activities that we know are counterproductive and bad for us, e.g. excessive drinking, smoking, gossiping, watching mindless TV, laziness, eating junk food etc. We know these things are bad for us, but they are also quite seductive. It actually takes an effort not to partake. There is a resistance to be overcome and therefore by limiting or eliminating our indulgence in such activities, we are again developing our mental strength.

The amount of mental strength developed by abstaining from activities depends upon how much control the activity in question has upon us. I've never really liked alcohol and as a result I don't drink. I don't experience any resistance when abstaining from drink and therefore my abstinence does not develop any mental strength (no resistance to overcome, no increase in strength).

By contrast, I have friends who in the past have struggled with alcoholism. Not drinking for them involves overcoming a huge resistance and their successful battle with the booze has therefore developed a large amount of mental strength. It may seem odd to some, but the greater the attraction we currently experience towards anything which is counterproductive or harmful, the greater the opportunity to develop our mental strength.

Cutting out the things that are bad for us not only improves our health and quality of life, it also develops our mental strength. Our weaknesses, through great effort, can be transformed into great strengths. That in no way means that these things are beneficial in themselves, because they are not. However, the process of removing them from our lives can be very beneficial. My friends who developed an addiction to drink have been made very strong by their eventual abstinence. Obviously, they would all rather they had not developed an addiction in the first place, but having done so, abstinence (because it is extremely difficult for them) has increased their mental strength.

It's not always about abstinence either. The discipline of regularly engaging in activities that are good for us and those around us can also bring about developments in mental strength. I've been training in the martial arts since I was a child. Those who also train in the martial arts will know that it is often a very hard and demanding experience. Regularly engaging in such training has not only made me a better martial artist, but it has also strengthened me mentally and improved the quality of my life.

In his book 'Karate-Do Nyumon' karate master Gichin Funakoshi wrote, 'One whose spirit and mental strength have been strengthened by sparring with a never-say-die attitude should find no challenge too great to handle. One who has undergone long years of physical pain and mental agony to learn one punch, one kick, should be able to face any task, no matter how difficult, and carry it through to the end. A person like this can truly be said to have learned karate.' It's not only the martial arts that can bring this kind of benefit, any activity which takes great effort is sure to develop our mental strength.

Engaging in demanding activities, taking regular exercise, getting to bed at a regular time, educating ourselves, taking the time to help and support others, all take effort and involve overcoming resistance. It would be easier not to do those things, but by overcoming the desire for inactivity or indifference, we develop our mental strength. Not only do we make a positive contribution to ourselves and those around us, but we also develop our mental strength and make ourselves more capable of achieving all the things we want from life.

Being self-centred and uncaring is easy. Caring about others requires effort. Anything that requires effort is capable of developing our mental strength. Not only is it right that we should do what we can to assist others, there is also something in it for us! By not taking the easy option and ignoring the problems of others, we gain the opportunity to develop ourselves mentally and hence bring good things into our own lives as well.

I believe that what goes around comes around. Some may see this as karma, reaping what you sow, or just the straightforward repercussions of social interaction (if you act like a jackass, people treat you like a jackass!). From whatever perspective you see it, there can be no doubt that if we behave in a negative way towards others, that negativity will find its way back to us. On the other hand, ensuring that our interactions with others are positive is a sure-fire way to ensure positive things will come into our own lives. We'll discuss this in more detail in the following chapter. For now, it sufficient to understand that making the effort to help others will bring positive things into your own life.

Before becoming a full-time writer and martial artist, I was employed as an electrician at a chemical plant. I'm a great believer in trade unions and the need for employees to have a collective voice. I was therefore very passionate and interested in union activities in my former place of work. A year or so after finishing my apprenticeship I was voted in as the shop steward for the thirty or so craftsmen who worked in the same part of the plant as myself. I knew it would be a difficult task (I was right!), but I also knew that this was an opportunity to help others.

During my decade as a shop steward, the relationship between myself and the management was generally cordial. On the whole, the management involved the representatives of the shop floor and listened to their concerns. This meant that in the majority of cases a way forward could be found that addressed the needs and concerns of all involved. However, there were times when serious issues needed to be addressed and conflicts arose. Emotions tend to run high during times of disagreement and as shop steward you're often the focal point for both the management's and the shop floor's frustrations.

Overall, I really enjoyed my time as a union activist. However, when things got very stressful, there were a number of times that I seriously considered quitting. In mental strength terms, the resistance I experienced promoted a desire to quit. By sticking with it and overcoming the desire to quit, I not only provided some small service to my fellow workers, but I also developed myself mentally.

Becoming a shop steward did not directly help me to become a full-time writer, but indirectly it definitely did. Not only did I gain a lot of experience that proved very useful when I went into business for myself (communication and negotiation skills, problem solving, how to treat people etc.), but I'd also enhanced my mental ability to endure difficult situations and see them through to the end. My time as a shop steward provided some mental cross-training that has since proved invaluable.

We have discussed that taking charge of our reactions to everyday situations, making the effort to avoid things which, although pleasurable, are harmful to us and engaging in activities that better ourselves and help others will all provide a resistance that can help to develop our mental strength and enhance the quality of our lives. Another type of resistance that can enter our lives is the personal tragedies and the upsetting and distressing events that most of us face at some point. It can be hard to see how such negative events can be beneficial, but they can. Obviously, we'd always much rather such events did not befall us or those around us, but if they do, and if we can get through to the other side, we will be much stronger people as a result.

I'd like to share with you a statement by the Chinese philosopher, Mencius: 'When heaven is about to confer an important office on a man, it first embitters his heart in its purpose; it caused him to exert his bones and sinews; it makes his body suffer hunger; it inflicts upon him want and poverty and confounds his undertakings. In this way it stimulates his will, steels his nature and thus makes him capable of achieving what would otherwise be impossible.'

What Mencius is saying is that there is positive benefit to be had in any tragedies that befall us. If we can get through those tragedies, the process of getting through to the other side will make us much stronger than we were, and we are therefore capable of achieving much more than we were. Indeed, Mencius seems to be saying that tragedy is the way in which heaven prepares us for greatness.

Another person who shared similar views on the positive aspects of tragedy was Friedrich Nietzsche. One of Nietzsche's most famous statements is 'That which does not kill us, serves to make us stronger.' Most people will have heard that line, even if they have never heard of Nietzsche himself. However, I have also seen that same statement translated as 'That which does not destroy us, serves to make us stronger.' To my mind, the second translation makes more sense.

Let us say that an event affects a person so badly that they become a shadow of their former self. They become withdrawn and insular. All self-confidence has been lost. Now that person has not been killed, but does that mean the event made them stronger? I think it is obvious that it does not. If the person has fought through the difficulties and eventually got to the point where the event had no negative effect on their lives, then that process will have made them much stronger. In the first instance we could argue that the former self has been destroyed. It is for this reason that I feel that the second translation is a more accurate one.

None of this means that personal tragedy is good or desirable. It obviously isn't. It just means that the challenging events that enter our lives have the potential to advance us. However, negative situations can only advance us if we make the determined effort to overcome them. As we have discussed throughout this book, the strength we need to overcome resistance is developed by attempting to overcome that resistance. In the event of a tragedy, the resistance may be so great that we'll need plenty of help and support to get though it. However, as long as we do get through it, we'll be stronger people as a result.

Many of the successful people that I know have had to overcome great difficulties in their lives. It's my view that the act of overcoming those difficulties developed their mental strength to such a degree that overcoming the proactive resistance they experience on the way to their goals was comparatively easy. They are used to facing challenges and overcoming difficulties and are therefore not afraid to face things head on. Nietzsche also wrote, 'Examine the lives of the best and most fruitful men and peoples, and ask yourself whether a tree, if it is to grow proudly into the sky, can do so without bad weather and storms.'

We need to experience resistance in our lives if we are to become mentally stronger and more able to live our lives as we wish. Hopefully, most of the resistance we experience will be the proactive resistance we have sought out as we make progress towards our goals. Some of the resistance will also come from the day-to-day events and temptations we all experience. And, unfortunately, sometimes that resistance will be caused by tragedy and other such wholly unwelcome events. Regardless of where it comes from, all resistance has the potential to make us stronger.

It is obviously very important to ensure that we expose ourselves to the specific resistances needed to advance us towards the goals we have set for ourselves. If we engage in the activities in which we wish to excel, the required resistances and challenges will naturally come our way so that we can develop both our mental strength and our talents. As we overcome these proactive resistances we will develop the specific skills and strengths needed to advance in accordance with the SAID principle. However, in our day-to-day lives it is also possible to use the challenges, difficulties, temptations and tragedies we face (everyday resistance) to further strengthen ourselves in a more general way.

Not only does overcoming everyday resistance increase our mental strength, it will also conserve our energies for the things that really matter, increase our discipline and self-control, enhance the quality of our daily lives, get us through our bad times, and help us to be of some assistance to our fellow man. The very act of being alive will provide numerous opportunities to develop our mental strength. Be sure to keep an eye out for them and always be ready for a bit of mental cross-training!

Chapter 10

Strength in Numbers

*'The most important single ingredient in the formula
of success is knowing how to get along with people'*
— Theodore Roosevelt

Whilst mental strength is an individual attribute, other people can affect the development of that strength and the potency of the resistances we face in both positive and negative ways. How we interact with the people around us will also significantly affect our ability to reach our goals. It is therefore very important that we interact with others in a way that will help us achieve our goals and is beneficial for all concerned. If our interactions with others are positive, we will progress towards our goals and grow stronger. Conversely, if we interact with others in a negative way we grow weaker and distance ourselves from our goals.

The first type of interaction we will look at is that of the spotter. In weightlifting, it is very common to have a training partner who will offer encouragement, give feedback on your lifting technique and ensure your safety. This training partner is known as a spotter. Chief among the spotter's tasks is to ensure that the weightlifter can work within the zone of development without overexerting themselves. Should the weightlifter end up being outside the zone of development, the spotter will assist by coming to the aid of the weightlifter and taking some of the load. The amount of help provided should be just enough to allow the weightlifter to continue to move the weight, without providing so much help that the weightlifter is no longer in the zone of development because the spotter is doing all the work!

As we progress towards our goals we may also come across spotters in the form of people who are prepared to help us by taking some of the strain. It can be very beneficial to your advancement if you can find someone who will provide guidance and encouragement, and help you along your chosen path. However, we need to ensure that those people don't help us too much!

This desire to avoid receiving too much help does not mean that we refuse the help of others, or that we have to take everything on ourselves. What it means is that we need to ensure that we personally experience enough resistance to develop our mental strength and talent. If our helpers remove that resistance, they also remove the opportunity to reach our true potential!

When I write a book, there are several people I ask to read it before it is put forward to the publishers. These close friends and family members will then provide me with their honest opinions of my work. If I agree with their opinions, I'll then rewrite certain sections of the book in order to make the book as readable and accessible as it can be. These people act as my literary spotters. Just like a spotter in the gym, they help me with the last little bit of the book in order for me to get as much out of it as I can. What they don't do is write the book for me, nor do they do the rewrites on my behalf! If they did, aside from the fact it would be very dishonest, they would deny me the opportunity to become a better writer.

As a further example, let's imagine that two people are both setting up their own business. Person A has a very wealthy relative who says that they will provide as much money as they need for the business for the first five years. Person B has no such financial backer. On the surface it may seem like Person A is more likely to end up with a successful business in the long term, but this may not be the case. Person A will experience very little resistance during the first five years of the business. As a result, they have little opportunity to develop their mental strength and their talent for business. There is no need to think creatively because they can throw money at every problem.

Person B is going to have to think very creatively in order to bring money into their business. They will need to make their business attractive to investors, and they will need a very robust and well thought out business plan to do so. They will need to ensure every penny spent is of maximum benefit to the business. Person B will become the better business manager because they have resistances to overcome. Person A is likely to struggle enormously when the free money runs out! They have received so much help that it has become a hindrance.

We all need a little help from time to time, and there is absolutely nothing wrong with that. However, if our helpers want to help so much that they do the job for us, they not only remove our resistance but they also remove our opportunities for advancement. Far from developing our strength and talents, we may become reliant on the strength and talents of the helper.

Our helpers should be like a good spotter in the gym. They are there to help us complete a given task when we truly can't push any further. If you have the opportunity, it may seem tempting to sit back and let others bring you your success (it's not really your success, it's theirs!). In the interest of our own development, we need to thank them for their offer, politely decline, tell them it's great to know that they are there for us if we need them, and then insist on how important it is to make our own way forward.

One thing to keep in mind is that the mentally strong generally want to promote mental strength in others. It is therefore quite unlikely that a truly strong person will provide too much help. They will always be there to offer support, encouragement and advice, and the mentally strong will always ensure that you don't 'drop the weight'. However, they won't do the job for you; they will instead help you to do the job yourself.

Excessive assistance is quite often the result of those who like to be liked, or the result of an excessive and misplaced desire to ensure that we are OK (e.g. an overprotective parent or friend). In both of these cases, the desire to help, although misplaced and ultimately counterproductive, is genuine in its intent. Another and perhaps more sinister reason why people can be excessively helpful is the desire (consciously or subconsciously) to keep others in a state of dependence. The person giving the help is effectively ensuring that we don't experience resistance and therefore we are unable to become mentally stronger or more talented. Because they shelter us from all resistance, we can't grow and can't achieve anything without their input. Whatever the reason, if we truly want to be successful, fulfilled and happy, we can't allow people to take away our challenges.

Whilst we need to ensure that we personally experience enough resistance to keep ourselves in the zone of development, there is nothing wrong with receiving genuine help. Needing help is often incorrectly seen as a sign of weakness. However, genuine help can be a very important part of our development.

We'll now move on to look at the types of help we can receive that are beneficial to our development. The first situation we will look at is when we find ourselves on the wrong side of our zone of development.

As we discussed in Chapter Three, in order to develop mental strength in the optimum way, we need to overload ourselves by just the right amount (be in the zone of development). If we don't overload ourselves enough, we don't grow. If we overload ourselves too much, we will overstress ourselves and again we won't grow. In our quest to better ourselves and achieve our goals, there may come a time when we find we've reached a little bit further than we should. What we thought was achievable turns out to be beyond us at that moment in time. In short, we bit off more than we could chew.

This often happens to me with my weight training. When I've strengthened myself to the point where lifting a certain weight is no longer beneficial (now inside my comfort zone), I need to increase the weight. I freely admit that sometimes my ambition, perhaps even my ego, encourages me to increase the weight by a little bit more than perhaps I should. Sometimes I surprise myself and have comparatively little trouble lifting the increased weight. Other times I realise that I'm not yet ready for that level! That's when I ask for help (normally by grunting loudly and contorting my face!). My spotter will then come to my aid and save me from injuring myself. I can then continue to lift that weight with my spotter's help, or to safely abandon the lift and reduce the weight to a more productive level.

When we do find that we've stretched ourselves a little too far, or that circumstances have conspired to place us on the wrong side of the zone of development, we should never be averse to asking for help. The help of others may just lighten the load enough to place us back into the zone of development, and ensure that the task gets completed. If the task is still too great, the assistance of others may allow us to make a tactical retreat back into our developmental zone with the minimum of complications. Either of these outcomes will ultimately develop our mental strength and allow us to expand our capabilities. If we refuse to ask for help, in the misguided belief that to do so is an indication of weakness, we remain overloaded and the situation is less likely to have a positive or beneficial outcome.

When I started to publish my first book I had absolutely no idea about the publishing process. It was obvious that I was going to have to move out of my comfort zone (no book publishing skills were to be found within that zone!). I bought a book on publishing and that gave me enough knowledge to get started. Having read those books, my knowledge had grown, but was still not enough to get the actual book into print. I had decided that I wanted the book to be printed before the end of the year and hence I needed to make progress pretty quickly. My lack of understanding and my self-imposed deadline meant that I was out of my depth and was experiencing resistance beyond the zone of development. I essentially had two options: to extend my deadline and give myself more time to develop my knowledge, or to get help. I decided to stick to my original deadline and to get some help.

I talked to authors, publishers, typesetters, printers, librarians, photographers and all kinds of people who worked in the publishing industry. I asked them to explain the bits of the process that I couldn't understand. In some cases I asked them if they could do certain tasks that were definitely beyond me (e.g. the typesetting). Almost everyone I talked to was extremely helpful and as a result the publication of the book began to progress. The act of publishing a book was still outside my comfort zone, but with the help of others I was able to stay within the zone of development (and learn lots!). They helped me overcome the resistance that I was not able to overcome on my own. As a result I found myself able to cope with a very steep learning curve, the book was published on time and, most importantly, I was able develop my knowledge and talent.

In any endeavour it makes sense to forge relationships with those whose skills, strengths and goals complement your own. These relationships will normally be in the form of either mutual support or coaching. First, we'll look at mutual support.

For us to progress in any field of endeavour we are sure to need the support and skills of others. To give a basic example, I'm currently pressing keys on my keyboard in order to write this book. I also need this computer to prepare the book for printing. I know next to nothing about computers, but I need a working computer with functioning software in order to produce my books. Although related to my chosen goal, being able to write software etc. is not one of the goals I've set for myself. And that's OK because there are others who can do that for me.

In order for my business to prosper, I also need the help of many other people who have skills that I do not. As a writer, it's my job to write, but in order to do that writing I need the help of editors, printers, publishers, sales teams, accountants, artists, photographers, proof-readers, magazine editors, computer programmers, web-designers, book stores, etc. Without the support of the people around me I'd be unable to write for a living.

The flipside of the support I receive from others is that they also need support from me (and other authors). I provide the material that the printers print, the books that the sales team sell, the articles that feature in the magazines, the money for the accountant to organise etc. We effectively support one another and ensure that we are all successful as a whole. There is no doubt that collective strength is greater that individual strength, and that we can achieve a lot more by working together than we could on our own.

The effect of mutual support is seen in practically all activities. A painter can't produce good works of art if a chemical company does not produce good quality paint. A sportsman can't play to the best of his ability if sports companies don't produce good quality equipment. A musician won't sound good without someone to manufacture high-quality instruments. There can be little doubt that, whatever our goal, we will need to call upon other people to provide the strengths and skills that support our own. Likewise, there will come a time when they will need to call upon us.

Mutual support may be based on something as simple as money: we need their skills, and they require the money that our own skills have generated, or vice-versa. However, mutual support can also be based on the common desire to achieve related goals. A good example of this is my martial arts sparring partners. By training together and working against one another we can all develop our martial skills. It is in our interests to ensure that we all improve as much as possible so that we can continually challenge each other and therefore ensure continual development.

In my business dealings I've surrounded myself with great people who understand that my success will, in turn, help them to be more successful. Likewise, the more successful they are, the more successful I'm likely to be. It's never going to be a productive relationship in the long term, for either party, if one side is only concerned about what's in it for them.

A relationship that will be productive for all concerned will always involve mutual support. Through that mutual support, both parties will be able to advance. If the people around me prosper, then they are in a better position to help me prosper also. Sadly some people adopt the attitude of just looking out for themselves. So long as they're OK, then everything is OK. On the surface the 'me, me, me' attitude would seems to have benefit for the person doing all the taking, but nothing could be further from the truth.

Let's take the example of a businessman who has no regards for those around him and only cares about how much money he is making. He reluctantly pays his suppliers at the last minute. He pays his staff the absolute minimum and is constantly pressurising them to do more and more. He also doesn't care about his customers' needs; he only cares about how much money he can extract from them.

Initially the miserly businessman will probably make a little more money than he would if he considered the needs of those around him. However, in the long term, it is very doubtful that his business will be successful. His suppliers won't value his custom. His staff will feel no sense of loyalty towards him and will always be looking to leave for a more enjoyable, more rewarding job. Word will also spread about his attitude to his customers and he will certainly lose business. If he cared about his suppliers' businesses, they are more likely to care about his business and hence they could work together to find ways where they can both make money. If he treats his staff well, they are more likely to reciprocate and go the extra mile to ensure the business is a success. If he looks after his customers' needs and always tries to give them what they need (not what makes him the most money), word will spread and he is sure to get more business. It's always in our own interest to care about those around us.

If you're not interested in the well-being of those around you, they are unlikely to be interested in yours. However, we shouldn't just care about those who can immediately give something back to us. We also need to care for those who, on the surface, would seem to have nothing to offer in return. Everything is related to everything else to a lesser or greater degree and therefore providing assistance to anyone is likely to bring us a positive result, eventually.

The world is a big place and it can sometimes take a while before our good deeds find their way back to us. This can sometimes make us think that, because we didn't get an immediate payoff from the person we assisted, mutual support isn't working and we'd have been better off by simply looking after number one. If we do something to help others it will always find its way back to us eventually.

To take a simple example, let's say that we help someone and as a result they are in a really good mood. Emotions can be infectious and therefore everyone they interact with will also get a dose of that positivity. The good mood we created will spread, and sooner or later it may find its way back to us. There is a hidden network at work that always ensures we get what we deserve. If we do positive things for others, positive things will find their way into our lives. Conversely, if we affect others in negative ways, negative things will find their way back to us. Sometimes what goes around will come around in a very direct, immediate and obvious way. Other times it will be much more subtle; however, what we put out will always find its way back to us.

Whilst many can see the benefit in looking after those who will also look after them, some can't grasp the subtle interactions and events that dictate the need to care about those with nothing to offer. They can't see where the mutual support is if the person they're helping has nothing they need.

Every positive act we perform makes the world a more positive place for ourselves and everyone else. Sometimes we can't see this subtle web at work and therefore we put things down to luck, fate or coincidence. However, every event has a cause. A negative cause will have a negative effect. A positive cause will have a positive effect. Sooner or later, our actions are likely to find their way back to us. We can't control all the variables in life, but we need to ensure that the ones we can control are likely to bring us good things. If we always endeavour to support those around us, we are unlikely to find ourselves lacking support and are far more likely to find ourselves on fate's good side.

Acting in a positive way is likely to bring positive situations and people into our lives; however, acting in a negative way will repel those exact same people and situations. In order for mutual support to work as effectively as possible, it is vital that we have the best people around us. Positive people know this and hence they also want other positive people around them. If we are negative and self-centred in our dealings with others, we inadvertently tend to push the people we need away from us. If we are positive towards all those around us, we naturally attract the right people into our lives.

We all live on the same planet and it is therefore my view that we all have an obligation to our fellow residents. If we all took the time to consider how our actions and inactions impacted on others, the world would be a much better place for all of us.

The people who only care about themselves often fail to see that it is in their own self-interest to care for others. They live in a little 'positive' bubble where the suffering of others never enters their mind and hence they incorrectly believe it has no effect upon them. As we have already said, everything affects everything else and all negativity, however seemingly remote, will always have an effect on our lives. I'm not saying that we should carry the weight of all the problems of the world on our shoulders, just that we should do what we can, and never blank out the suffering of others or accept the unacceptable.

You don't have to become heavily involved in politics to make a contribution, and opinions always vary on the best solution for every problem. However, the little steps we can all take do add up to make a big difference: pop some spare change in charity boxes, be prepared to challenge any injustices you experience, use your vote and encourage others to do likewise, and so on. My wife, who is a very caring woman, makes a positive contribution through our day-to-day shopping. Large companies also have a large influence and my wife endeavours to support those companies that make the most positive contribution to the greater good. She has educated herself about the activities and policies of various companies and therefore is prepared to spend money with some, and none with others. Whatever positive actions we take, regardless of whether they are big or small, they will all make a positive difference to the world around us.

To recap, the act of considering the needs of those around you ensures that you'll have people around you who will be able to provide the help, guidance and assistance you need. To make the maximum progress, we need the best possible people around us. If you make the effort to become the kind of person people like to have around, you'll always have the best people around you. Also, we need to understand that every action we make, positive and negative, will eventually make its way back to us and will have a wider impact than we often realise. Finally, caring about others involves overcoming mental resistance. This resistance takes the form of a desire to take the easy path and just look out for number one. When we attempt to care about others, we need to use our mental strength to overcome that resistance. Whatever requires mental strength can develop mental strength; therefore, caring about others also has the positive benefits of making us stronger!

Having discussed mutual support and the positive benefits that caring about others can bring, I'd like to move on to discuss another form of support that can effect our mental strength and ability to progress, that of coaching.

In order to develop our talent and skills it is almost inevitable that we will need to learn from those who are further advanced than ourselves. To develop as a martial artist, I need to study under those whose skills are more advanced than my own. To progress as a writer, I need to learn from people who are more experienced than I am in all things literary. Whatever your chosen field, you'll need to seek out the help and tuition of those who possess the skills, strengths and talents that you desire.

In order to be as good as you can be, it is important to learn from the best people that you can find. If you learn from someone who has mediocre skills themselves, the best you can really hope for is to be mediocre yourself. That is why it is very important to learn from people who are successful in your chosen field. Every subject has an army of armchair experts and their advice, although well meaning, is often incorrect. Be sure that you always seek the guidance and teaching of people who have been there and done that.

As we have already discussed, it is the advice and guidance of the skilled and successful that is most valuable to us. It has been my experience that those who are skilled and successful had to learn from others themselves and they are therefore generally not averse to sharing their knowledge. In most cases, all you need to do in order to learn from others is to ask for their help, and then listen to what they have to say. However, there will be times when people won't be prepared to teach you.

There are a few different reasons why people won't share their knowledge or teach. The first and most obvious reason is that they may simply not have the time or inclination to teach you. If this is the case, then find someone who is prepared to teach you.

One other reason that people won't teach you is that you're not yet up to the required level. When seeking out tuition, you need to earn the right to be taught by people at the elite level. As an example, I haven't played tennis since I left school (wasn't any good at it then). If I was to now decide that I want to be a world-level player, it is very unlikely that a world-level coach would be interested in teaching me! What I should do is seek out the best local coach that I can. Once I've developed a good fundamental skill level and had some local success, I'm more likely to be accepted by a national level coach. From there, I could eventually progress beyond national level and find myself being taught by a world-level coach. Just like all other aspects of advancement, it's important not to overreach or undersell yourself. Whatever your chosen field, you need the best instruction and guidance that your current level affords you access to.

Another of the more common reasons for people being unwilling to teach is that the pupil is not yet ready to learn. By 'not ready to learn' I mean that the pupil likes the idea of learning, or they may like the association with their prospective teacher, but they have no real desire to listen and take onboard any advice or guidance given. To be successful, you have to be busy and active. When you are busy and active, you won't want to waste time on those who ask for guidance, but then don't listen to that guidance when it is given.

There is a famous story about a well-educated man who goes to visit a monk in order to discuss spiritual matters. The monk begins to prepare a drink of tea whilst the well-educated man repeatedly asks him a question and then, before the monk has time to answer, informs the monk of his own views and opinions on the subject they are discussing. After a few minutes of this the monk begins to pour the tea into his cup. The cup fills up, starts to spill over the sides, and yet the monk keeps on pouring. As the tea spills all over the table, the well-educated man finally asks the monk to stop and asks him what he is doing. The monk explained that the man's mind was like the cup and was full to the brim with knowledge. There was no room for anything new! The monk explained further, that if the man was to learn anything from him, he should 'empty his cup' of his views, opinions and preconceptions and simply listen to what the monk had to say.

It's very difficult to teach someone if they don't really want to learn! When we ask people for advice and guidance, they are always much more likely to give that advice if they think we really want it. If it is apparent that all we really want to do is proudly show off our own knowledge, then we are effectively wasting the time of both ourselves and the person whose guidance we asked for. If we truly want the guidance of those who have progressed further than ourselves, and we ask for that guidance with a genuine humility, you'll be amazed at how much people will share with you.

For my part, I've been teaching the martial arts for around seventeen years now. During that time, it's not the students with natural ability that have proved the most satisfying to teach, but the ones with the most enthusiasm for the arts. I was never a natural myself, but I had a burning enthusiasm and a strong desire to learn, which ensured I made good progress. I now recognise that same enthusiasm in others. It's definitely the ones with genuine enthusiasm who progress the furthest and hence they're the ones I prefer to teach.

Anyone who is highly successful in any given field must have a great passion for it. It's this passion that will fuel the development of their mental strength and give them the energy to overcome all the obstacles they will face. Successful people generally love being around those who share their passions. I have a great passion for the martial arts and hence I really enjoy spending time with those who share that passion, whether they are my peers, my students or my seniors. In whatever area you choose to excel, you'll find that those who are more successful than you will be very happy to help you progress if they recognise your genuine love of the field. A genuine desire to learn and a strong enthusiasm will open a lot of doors.

Another reason people can be reluctant to teach us is that we ask too much from them. At the beginning of this chapter we discussed how the people that wish to help us can actually become a hindrance if they take away so much resistance that we are no longer in the zone of development. You'll also recall that the mentally strong are generally very aware of this fact and want to encourage growth in others. They are therefore very unlikely to help those who want too much from them, because to do so would be counterproductive. If the pupil is overly dependant on those they ask for guidance, they will not benefit from the guidance and hence both the teacher's and student's time will be wasted.

The most common reason that a pupil will ask for too much is that they like the idea of being skilled and knowledgeable, but they are reluctant to overcome the resistance that they personally experience. They want the teacher to do the job for them!

Many of the instructors and teachers I know (of martial arts and other disciplines) have at one time or another had a pupil who demanded far too much from them. They may really like the idea of being good at a particular skill, but they do not wish to put in the required work. They are unable to discipline themselves and therefore always expect the instructor to provide their discipline. They are unable to motivate themselves and therefore expect the instructor to always provide their motivation. They don't make the effort to retain information or internalise technique and therefore always expect the instructor to show them the same things over and over. In short, they take no responsibility for their own learning. A good instructor will do whatever they can to make the pupil aware of their lack of responsibility and help them to move past it. However, if the pupil is unwilling to move beyond this dependant mindset, teaching them becomes a waste of time. No one wants to teach a pupil like this.

If we approach people, with a genuine desire to learn, they will generally be only too happy to coach us. Be sure to seek out guidance and instruction from the most experienced and willing teachers. If you're willing to learn from those who have the skills you require, and they are in turn genuinely interested in passing those skills on to you, you are sure to make strong progress.

We should also remember that we don't always have to learn from someone in person; although that is definitely the best way. It is also possible to learn from the written material of those who have excelled in your chosen field. You can gain a great deal from reading. As I've already mentioned, I acquired the knowledge I needed to get started in publishing from a book. I also taught myself to typeset from books. In both cases I also called upon the guidance of those experienced in those fields, but the knowledge gained from reading those books proved to be invaluable. Reading can be one other way in which you can learn from others and increase your knowledge, skills and talent.

The flip side of learning from others who have progressed further than ourselves is that we must also be prepared to teach those who ask us for our guidance when we achieve success. Not only is it right that you should help people in the same way that others helped you, but it is also in your own interest to do so. It is important to spend time around people who share our interests and goals. We can draw inspiration from those above us, from our peers, and from the determination and enthusiasm of those who make the climb behind us. You'll find you'll get a lot of energy from teaching others and this will help you to make further progress yourself.

Teaching others also benefits your chosen field. If you have a genuine enthusiasm and love for your field of endeavour – which you need if you're going to progress – you'll not only care about your own advancement, but the advancement of the field itself. As more people get involved and strive for greatness within that field, the more the field itself will advance.

It can sometimes be tempting to view those with similar goals to ourselves as competitors and therefore we could question the wisdom of helping them to succeed. There are several reasons why this mindset can be self-defeating. The main one is that being fearful of the success of others indicates a lack of mental strength. On some level you must doubt your own skills and strengths if you believe others can take what you have away from you. This negative thinking is just another form of mental resistance that must be overcome in order to develop true strength within ourselves. True success and true strength are never dependant upon the failures of others.

Another reason why we should help others to succeed is that it will help our chosen field to progress and that in turn will help our own progression. The first few books I wrote were about the application of the forms found within the traditional martial arts. Since those books were published, I've been fortunate enough to help a number of others get their own books and articles published on the subject of form applications. Some could argue that I would have been better not to help them as there are now more books and articles in competition with my own, but that's not how I see it.

Because more people have got their books and articles published, information on the subject is now more widely available. I have a love of the traditional arts (and the modern ones too for that matter) and therefore I'm delighted to have done something that helps disseminate information on them. However, in addition to serving the interests of others and the art itself, my own interests are also served. Because there is more information out there, interest in the field inevitability grows. And because interest in the field has grown, I sell more books! It is always in our own interests to help others.

Let's suppose that we help others to succeed, and they do so to the point where they become serious competitors and surpass our own level such that our work is less valued or we lose business. Again, some would see our assistance as being to our own detriment. However, in my view this apparently negative situation is actually very beneficial to us. As we have discussed throughout this book, in order to advance we need to experience resistance. If there are no obstacles and resistance, there can be no growth. Our competitors, whether self-created or not, can provide that resistance and are therefore something we need to progress (more on that in the next chapter). Another positive aspect to our being surpassed by those we helped is that they are now in a position to help us! In the vast majority of cases they will not be averse to affording us the same help we afforded them and we have then created a situation of mutual support.

The final way in which helping others to surpass ourselves can be of benefit to us is that our help is sure to become highly valued! Others will see what our guidance and instruction has achieved and will want it themselves. This will help bring more people into our lives who share our goals and who we can draw energy from.

I know there will still be plenty of people who will question the wisdom of aiding potential competitors, and that's great! It's important to think for yourself and come to your own conclusions. All I can say is that I firmly believe that it's always in your own self-interest to help others. I don't say this from a moral standpoint, but more from the position of my own experience. All the help I've received, and all the help I've given to others has always helped me to advance. On a personal note, I also want every achievement I have to be earned through my own sweat and toil; it would mean nothing to me otherwise. I want my achievements to be honest and true. Withholding information from others, or hampering the advancement of others in any other way, in an attempt to maintain or advance my position, would rob me of all sense of accomplishment. For me, that's far too high a price to pay.

So far in this chapter, we've looked at how people who want to help us, or who share our goals, can affect our progress and development. We've also discussed that being around those who share our enthusiasm for our chosen field can also inspire us and give us energy. However, we can also draw energy from being around anyone who has a strong desire to advance, regardless of what field they wish to advance in. I have a friend who is a very talented artist. I have no interest in advancing myself as a painter, but seeing his work and observing his determination and work ethic is a huge inspiration to me. I have quite a few friends who are successful in areas that I have no real interest in myself, but seeing their success always fills me with energy and makes me more determined to achieve my own goals. It is definitely very important to spend time around encouraging, energetic and inspiring people.

Being around strong and successful people will definitely help you to succeed. In the same way that a weightlifter is careful to only eat the foods that will enhance his strength and health, we need to be sure that we only take things into our minds that will increase our mental strength. Being around strong people will ensure we have positive influences all around us and provide positive mental nourishment.

If your current environment does not give you access to the company of inspirational people (it will when you start to advance), then there are plenty of other ways in which you can draw energy from others. Read inspiring books, watch inspiring films, listen to inspiring music etc.

I've found that teaching the martial arts involves quite a bit of driving as I transport myself from one location to the next. I use the time to listen to inspiring radio programmes (interviews with strong and successful people), inspirational spoken-word tapes and inspirational music. What we find inspirational is definitely a matter of personal taste. For me, the bulk of what I class as inspirational music is punk-rock (high-energy songs, many of which emphasise the dangers of being seduced by mediocrity, the need to consider the plight of others, and the joys of walking a path less travelled). Punk is the music I grew up on, but I fully understand that it is not everyone's cup of tea. Whatever you find gives you the energy to advance, be sure to draw energy from it on a regular basis.

In this chapter we've discussed how other people can help you to become stronger and advance. There is definitely strength in numbers and we should do what we can to ensure that our interactions with others are always beneficial for ourselves and everyone else.

Although we may make the effort to ensure that our interactions with others are beneficial, other people may not make that same effort. It is therefore always a possibility that other people may behave in a way that has the potential to damage us or hinder our progress. Although we can't control the actions of others, we can control our reaction to their behaviour and the effect it has. In the next chapter, we'll look at the role of the enemy and explain why those who attempt to hinder our advancement also have an important role to play in our development.

Chapter 11

Foes and Enemies

*'It is not the critic who counts; not the man who points
out how the strong man stumbles, or where the doer of
deeds could have done them better. The credit belongs to
the man who is actually in the arena, whose face is
marred by dust and sweat and blood'*
– Theodore Roosevelt

In any endeavour we are likely to come across people who, intentionally or unintentionally, behave in ways that have the potential to hinder our progress. This behaviour can range from an off-the-cuff remark that could rob us of our confidence, through to deliberate attempts to sabotage our endeavours. We can't control the actions of others. However, if we have sufficient mental strength, we can control how we respond to their actions and control the effects that those actions have. In this chapter we will look at the various negative actions that people can take, and how we can address these actions so that they have a positive effect.

The first type of potentially harmful behaviour that I'd like to look at is friendly fire. By friendly fire I mean the behaviour of others that is potentially harmful without meaning to be. In fact, in many cases those engaging in such behaviour genuinely believe that they are acting in your best interests. Even though their motivation may be friendly, their actions are your 'foe'.

I can recall getting ready for one of my early karate gradings (an exam to see if I was ready to pass onto the next belt). I had trained pretty hard for the exam and was feeling pretty confident about my chances of passing. As I left the house to make my way to the dojo (karate training hall), one of my relatives said to me, 'Best of luck Iain. Try not to be too disappointed if you fail.' I have no doubt that the words of my relative were said with the best of intentions, but those words revealed that they suspected I was not up to the task. They were worried that I was setting myself up for a fall and would be upset if it became apparent that I'd overreached myself. As it transpired, I passed with the highest marks possible. Were it not for that fact that I knew how hard I'd worked, and that I was profoundly stubborn as a teenager, those well-meaning, if misguided words could easily have robbed me of my confidence and therefore sabotaged my performance at my grading.

Another, more recent example of friendly fire was when I decided to quit my day job and become a full-time writer and martial artist. A close friend told me that he was glad I'd had the courage to make such a bold move and that he was fully behind me (so far so good!). He then continued, 'And if it doesn't work out you can always go back to working as an electrician.' Again, I have no doubt that he had the best of intentions. However, his words revealed that he considered there was a very real possibility that my career as a writer and martial artist could fail. At that stage in my life, I had developed absolute certainty that I (and anyone else) can achieve anything so long as they truly believe they can and they fully intend to do so. If I'd placed store in his fallback plan that would mean that I too had less than a 100 percent conviction that I could achieve the goals I'd set for myself. In turn, this would dramatically reduce my ability to achieve those goals. Thankfully, I now find it relatively easy to fend off such friendly fire.

When I did leave the day job behind, one of my colleagues told me that I was sure to regret making such a reckless decision, that I should appreciate the job I had, and that he really wished I would think it through more carefully. He also told me that he hoped he was not out of place for encouraging me to reconsider what he thought was a reckless decision. Again, I have no doubt of the sincerity of his intentions, but his words could really have undermined my confidence and convinced me to play it safe had I not understood the nature of friendly fire.

I'm sure you'll have also come across plenty of examples of friendly fire in your own life (e.g. 'Be sure not to get your hopes up too high' etc.). One of the most common motivations for such behaviour is that the person concerned has a genuine concern for our well-being. However, that concern is often misplaced and tells you much more about their fears than it does about your abilities.

Most people fear for others what they fear for themselves. If a person is scared of something, they feel fearful for others when they see them confronting that something. For example, my old colleague who told me that he considered my decision to become a full-time writer to be very reckless had always aimed for a secure job. He feared change and risk, and hence he desired the security that our jobs offered. Losing or leaving that job would expose him to change and risk. Therefore he worried about my being exposed to the change and risk that he himself feared.

When friendly fire does come your way it's important to deal with it correctly. There are two key things to remember. Firstly, that the person making those comments, even though they are potentially damaging, probably has nothing but a genuine, if misguided concern for your well-being. Secondly, remember that their comments reveal far more about their own fears than they do about your abilities. In my experience, the best way to deal with friendly fire is to thank the person for their concern, and then explain that, although you fully understand their intention was to help, their statement could undermine your confidence if you allowed it to. Explain that you firmly believe yourself to be up to the task, that you fully intend to go ahead, and in doing so you'd appreciate their support. If the person continues to fire negativity in your direction, be sure to ignore it and remember that their misplaced concern says more about them than you.

It is very important not to allow yourself to think negatively when pursuing your goals (or at any other time for that matter). If you allow negative thoughts to rattle around your brain your performance will be affected in a negative way. Negative thoughts are like computer viruses. They can have a very negative effect on what would otherwise be a very efficient system. And like computer viruses, negative thoughts spread very rapidly! You must always remain focused and positive and not allow any friendly fire to introduce negative thoughts into your way of thinking. It's OK that negative thoughts appear (it's a sign you're making progress) but they should never be given the opportunity to hang around and have an effect.

I'm a great believer that our mental state can have a significant effect upon our physical health. If we're in a positive frame of mind, our bodies are healthier and work better. A while ago I damaged my left knee while practising throwing techniques. Because I was in pain and was unable to stand up, I went to the hospital where it was confirmed that I'd sustained some damage to my knee joint. I was convinced that I would heal quicker if I believed I would. It was therefore vital to ensure that no negative thoughts got a foothold.

A significant number of friends, family members and colleagues kept telling me that I'd need to take it very easy for a long time, that these things take time to heal, that I'd have to take great care with my knee from now on, that it would never be right again etc. All these comments, although well meaning, inferred that my injury was debilitating and would have a long-term or permanent effect. I was on the receiving end of friendly fire! I'm always sensible when I'm recovering from an injury, but I know I heal fast and I was 100 percent certain the knee would be as good as new. In order to facilitate the healing process, I needed to rebut the friendly fire that came my way. I told everyone who enquired about my injury that it was healing great and that I'd be back to full strength soon. It wasn't long before I no longer needed to strap the joint and was back training (very lightly at first). I firmly believe that had I succumbed to friendly fire the healing process would have taken much longer.

We must always be on the lookout for friendly fire, in whatever form, and ensure that it is never allowed to affect our frame of mind, our self-image, our confidence or our performance.

In addition to well-intentioned friendly fire there always exists the possibility that the person making such comments is trying to manipulate you and is dressing up this manipulation in friendly words. You alone are able to judge if that is the case. However, it's important to remember that no one can control you unless you allow them to. If you're resolute in your desire to reach your goals, people who try to dissuade you from doing so are unable to have any negative effect.

It is never a nice experience when someone acts in a negative way toward us. It's even more unpleasant when these actions are deliberate in their intent to undermine us and sabotage our ambitions. Most people will be supportive or indifferent towards your ambitions. However, there may be some who would like nothing more than to see you fail. Whatever their motivation may be, there may be times when you will have to deal with those who would set themselves up as your enemy.

It is very important to understand that people who revel in the failure of others are of limited development. By this I mean that they are extremely unlikely to have made any progress towards any of the things in life they would like to achieve. They are not the person they'd like to be, nor are they living the life they want to live. They generally feel completely helpless and powerless to change their situation and firmly believe that they are at the mercy of the world around them. It is for this reason that the failure of others feels like a comparative success. It may be tempting to feel animosity towards such people, but this is not really appropriate and it is certainly not healthy.

If a person is at a very low level of development (mentally very weak) they are not in a position to have a positive effect on themselves or those around them whilst they stay at that level. Their best may be a momentary feeling of esteem when they see others fall. When other people are successful, it reminds them of their own failings and the unhappiness of their current situation. The failure of others therefore gives them a brief respite from their feelings of inadequacy and helplessness. I certainly don't say that as a means to belittle those who would like to see us fail, but so that we can understand that their actions rarely have anything to do with a genuine animosity towards us and more to do with their own issues and the bleak way in which they view the world around them. It should be understood that they are doing the best they can with what they have.

When people behave in a way that is deliberately meant to harm us, we often experience a desire to inflict harm straight back. However, when we understand that people normally attack others from a position of weakness, it becomes obvious that it is not appropriate to retaliate. Those who are mentally strong will never feel threatened by those who are mentally weak. It is also very unlikely that those weaker than ourselves will actually be able to inflict any meaningful harm unless we allow them to. It is only when we lower ourselves to their level that their words and actions can have any real effect.

When we do find ourselves in someone's line of fire, the best defence and greatest show of strength is complete indifference. They can shout, scream, spread rumours, try to turn others against you, try to undermine you, but none of it has any effect. You're simply far too strong! All their negativity is like water off a duck's back. You don't even take a second to acknowledge the tiny arrows fired your way. You just keep on marching towards your goals. If you were to retaliate, you would lower yourself to their level (a level of weakness). If you were to allow it to have any effect, you would again submit to weakness. Instead use their negativity as an opportunity to flex and further develop your own mental strength.

When negative people try to undermine you, and because of your strength their actions have no effect, you may find that they will attack you with even greater ferocity. And that's fine, because that won't have any effect either! It's also a sign that their behaviour won't last forever (paradoxically, your doing nothing is having an effect!). Sooner or later they will blow themselves out.

I acknowledge that not reacting to the negative actions of others requires a huge amount of self-control and mental strength; however, isn't that what we're aspiring to? It should always be remembered that whatever requires strength also has the ability to develop strength. Indifference is not only strategically the best course of action; it is also the most beneficial.

If you truly can't get rid of the thought that you need to get even (and you should try hard to get rid of it) then perhaps you can take some solace from the fact that your inaction and self-control will drive the negativity spreaders crazy! They want to provoke a reaction and they want to have an effect. Tough luck! You're not going to give them what they want. No one can control you but you. Just completely ignore them and keep on moving onwards and upwards. When the desire to settle the score subsides, you'll see that there never really was a score to settle in the first place as their actions and words have had no effect on you whatsoever.

When I was younger the idea of turning the other cheek and not reacting when others attacked me was a difficult concept for me to accept. If someone took a shot at me, then it seemed only right that I should take a shot right back. I subscribed to the Machiavellian idea that people were more likely to treat you fairly if they fear the consequences of any negative action towards you. As I grew older it became more apparent that there was a higher level of strength. There was no need to adopt an eye for an eye approach if you had no fear of the actions of others. If you're so strong that people are unable to harm you or hinder your progress, you have no reason to fear them or have any concern about their actions towards you. The highest show of strength is complete indifference. There would be no feelings of fear or any need for vengeance. The wind can howl all it likes, the mountain won't move.

There is of course a difference between people's verbal attacks and those of a more tangible nature. If the attack can have a physical effect, i.e. an effect in the real world, then it is wise to neutralise that effect. For example, if someone attempts to physically harm you, then you need to remove yourself from the situation and failing that, you need an effective physical response. If the negative actions of others can have a real effect then you have to deal with those effects in the appropriate manner. However, in the vast majority of cases, the negative actions of others amount to nothing more than bluff and bluster. If we can put our egos to one side and look at the situation objectively, it will be plainly apparent in the vast majority of situations that these negative actions will have no real effect.

There are times when we can perceive people's actions or words as personal attacks when they are in fact nothing of the kind. The most common example of this is when we find ourselves on the receiving end of another's criticism. As you make progress toward your goals you are bound to catch the attention of others, many of whom will have an opinion on your merits, your work, your ability, and you personally. As a general rule, we love it when people praise us, and hate it when people criticise us. However, it's an inevitable part of progress that people will develop an opinion about you, and having done so, they will then share that opinion with others.

When you find yourself being criticised, remember that it is a sure sign that you're making progress. As Oscar Wilde said, 'There is only one thing in the world that is worse than being talked about, and that is not being talked about.' Although it can be unpleasant when others have a negative opinion about you or your work, I agree with Mr Wilde that people having no opinion is worse. If people don't have a view on you, it essentially means they don't consider you to be of any relevance.

Whether people love you or loathe you, at least they are showing that they believe you and your work have an influence. It really does not matter what people are actually saying about you. If you care too much about the opinions of others you'll start living your life in a way that you believe will be most pleasing to most people. The fact is that you can never please everyone and the overriding concern must always be to be true to your own vision of a good and happy life (more on that in Chapter Twelve).

An accomplished author once told me that they knew they'd made it when they received their first piece of hate mail! I'm pleased to say that the vast majority of the mail I've received about my writing has been very positive and supportive. However, I too was similarly excited when I attracted criticism with my martial arts books. There have been a few occasions where some in the martial arts world have been quite scathing about me and my work. Aside from informing me that my influence was growing, it also helped the sales of my books! Strange I know, but that's what happened. In fact I can honestly say that those who were the most virulent about me and my books helped sales almost as much as those who endorsed my work!

Whilst we should never go out of our way to upset people or court controversy, it's an inevitable consequence of having an opinion. There will always be some people who have a differing opinion and will want to convince others that your opinion is wrong! As a citizen of a democratic country where people are permitted to have differing opinions, I think that's great! If I want to express my own views and live my life my own way, I also have to accept that others are free to do the same; even if it means people disagree with my views or have contempt for me personally. Just do your own thing. If it provokes a positive reaction, that's fine. If you provoke a negative reaction, then that's also fine. People having an opinion on what you do is a sure sign that you're making progress. Don't let the criticism of others affect you, otherwise you are effectively giving them control over you. Other people can never make you feel good or bad about yourself unless you allow them to.

Having established that criticism is an inevitable consequence of making progress, we need to discuss how to deal with it. In order to do this, we need to first understand that there are essentially two types of criticism. Firstly, we have criticism that is instructive or objective. This refers to an honestly held and objective opinion of you, your abilities and your work in order to help you improve or to inform others of your merits and shortfalls (in the opinion of the critic). The second form of criticism is when those making the comments have a vested interest in what others think about you. This type of criticism is therefore unlikely to be objective and will either be overly positive or negative depending upon what will most benefit those making the criticism.

Objective criticism can be a very useful tool to help us move forwards. As we said earlier, we tend to like it when people praise us, and not like it when people are critical about us.

However, we need to put our egos to one side and look at objective criticism in an objective way. The criticism of others can help us identify strengths upon which we can build and shortfalls which we can then address. Whilst it should always be remembered that criticism is nothing more than the opinions of others, it can sometimes help us see things to which we had previously been blind.

My progress in the martial arts is very dependant upon the criticism of others. I constantly get others to look at my performance and technique and suggest how they can be improved. Sometimes the opinions of others are positive, and this helps me to maintain, capitalise and build upon my strengths. Sometimes their opinions help me to see flaws so that I can then set about addressing them. If it wasn't for the criticism of others I would find it much harder to progress.

The opinions I receive about my writing also help me to improve. I've asked people to read over my work and suggest how it can be improved. I've had people contact me to say what they liked and disliked about what I've written. I've also had reviews appear in magazines that have taught me something about my writing and helped me to grow my talent. Whilst the objective criticism of others can sometimes be uncomfortable, it can be very useful.

The second type of criticism is when the person has a vested interest. When we find others expressing an opinion, we always need to consider if they have a vested interest in order to determine how valid their opinion is. As an example, let's say you've done a painting and you've asked a close friend for their views. It could be that your friend is the kind of person who always likes to please, and hence their comments are overly positive. They may tell you that they like the painting because that is what they believe you want to hear. Your friend has a vested interest – they want you to be happy – so their opinion is likely to be skewed by that vested interest. Conversely, let's say that a competitor, who doesn't particularly like you, also criticises the painting. There is a possibility that their opinion will be overly negative as they believe it is in their interests to undermine your confidence and your work.

When we find ourselves being criticised, we must always examine the motives of those doing the criticising in order to determine its value (critique the criticism, as it were). We need to examine the criticism with our own minds and see if we agree. Remember, criticism and praise are just other people's opinions; they are not cold hard facts. We need the mental strength to switch off our egos and our preconceived ideas and see if we can learn from the criticism.

As human beings, we tend to screen the opinions of others through our own beliefs. Again, this prevents the criticism from being used in an objective way. If we have a negative view of ourselves or our work, we often reject praise as we believe it is just others being nice or trying to get on our good side. Likewise if we develop an over-inflated sense of self-importance, or even arrogance about our attributes, we are often quick to reject the criticism of others even though there may be merit in that criticism. If you have a reasonable understanding of yourself and others, making use of criticism is relatively simple if you don't let that criticism upset you or any praise delight you.

At the extreme end of criticism with a vested interest is the ranting of those whose sole objective is to belittle you. Such criticism is very easy to spot as it is never objective and is nothing more than spittle and venom. As we discussed earlier, these types of attacks normally come from those who are lacking in mental strength and feel threatened by you in some way. Whilst it can be easy to react to such attacks, it's always better not to. If it's obvious to you that the person is not being objective, it will also be obvious to almost everyone else. Those who throw muck around always end up covered in muck themselves... and it is always better not to throw it back! Those who attack you without merit will reveal far more about themselves than they ever will about you. It's better not to waste your valuable time with them.

All of us are human and hence there is always the possibility that our strength and self-control may not be sufficient for an attack to have no effect. The words and actions of others may upset us, cause us to feel anger or undermine our confidence. It should be remembered that the actions of others can have no effect unless we allow them to have an effect. However, if we are unsuccessful in that regard and people do get under our skin, there are still many ways in which we can avoid retaliating and acting in a weak manner.

We've already discussed a couple of these ways. You may be able to stem your desire to act through understanding that your inactivity will not give your attacker the reaction they desire. You may also be able to inject a bit of humour into the situation. The wholly negative attacks of the weak can have no real effect if you don't take them seriously or place any store in them.

Another way in which you can fend off the negativity of others is to feed on it! If we are unable to summon enough strength to render the attacks of others irrelevant, it is likely that we will experience a strong desire to react or retaliate. This strong desire to act is a kind of fuel that we can use in both negative and positive ways. If we use it to attack our attacker, we are dropping to their level (a level of weakness) and it will do nothing to move us towards our goal. We have allowed the energy generated from the attack to have an extremely negative effect upon us. However, if that energy is present, we can also use it in a positive way. You don't directly attack your attacker, but instead use the energy they have given you to drive you towards your goal. Use that emotional energy to prove them wrong!

This redirection of energy is a weaker and far less beneficial response than no response whatsoever. Your attacker has still been able to control you and have an effect. However, you've used the strength you have to turn it into a positive effect. Although indifference is the greatest show of strength, this redirection of energy is infinitely preferable to allowing your attacker to have a negative effect.

In this chapter we've discussed how friends, foes and critics can influence our development in a negative way if we allow them to. We've also seen how these attacks are a sure sign of progress. We've looked at how we can deal with these attacks. We've also discussed how we can use the attacks of others to further enhance our strength. Key to all of this has been the understanding that the harsh, meaningless and unwarranted attacks of others almost always originate from their own weaknesses and fears. The truly strong will never attack you in that way as they have control over their fears and are prepared to eliminate their weaknesses.

Truly successful people will never tell you that you can't be successful. They know from first hand experience that you can be! A great actor isn't going to say you can't be an actor, because they are the living proof that you can be! It's only those who are too fearful to make the attempt themselves, or those who made a half-hearted attempt and then failed to put in sufficient work that will tell you that you can't be a success. The only possible exception to this rule is those who are 'successful' by default. They feel that they don't really deserve their success and hence feel threatened by those who could rise through the ranks and take it away from them. Such a person, although they may have the trappings of status, are neither mentally strong nor truly successful. Truly successful people don't feel threatened by others. Keep these facts in mind if others should try to distract you or stop you from achieving your goals.

You should treat the negative words of others in the same way you treat your own negative thoughts. Both are a sign of progress, both provide a resistance which can develop mental strength and both should be quickly dismissed so that they can't have a negative effect upon you. As a strong person, you're in control of your mind and your life. The words and actions of others have no effect upon the strong.

In this book we have seen how heading towards our goals in such a way that we remain in the zone of development is sure to bring us the resistance we need to make progress. This resistance will develop our strengths and talents to the point where we need to experience greater resistance if further progress is to be made. As we progress towards our goals, we are certain to find that those who attack us will grow in number and stature; and although it may not sound like it, this is a good thing!

By way of example let's follow the career of a fiction writer. When our writer first starts writing stories she will only be sharing them with friends and perhaps members of a local writing circle. The criticism she gets is therefore likely to be moderate and not very widespread. When her first novel gets published, the criticism is likely to be stronger (more people read it and the book has more influence). This will inevitability mean a growth in the number of negative comments she will receive (you can't please all the people all the time). This is a sure sign of progress! Also, the moderate criticism she received when she first started will have helped develop the mental strength needed to deal with the more abundant negativity at this higher level. When her fifth novel becomes a blockbuster movie, the number of people that criticise her work will be even greater. Previously she would not have attracted the attention of those with wider influence (newspaper and TV critics etc.) so the criticism will now be more widespread. Again, this is a positive sign of progress and the resistance will again prepare her for even greater levels of success.

As we grow, along with bringing more strength, success and happiness into our lives, we will also attract more foes. However, we need our foes and our obstacles in order to develop ourselves and make progress. Those who stand against us can help us to progress, so long as we approach them in a positive way. In the same way that the weightlifter needs the resistance of the weight in order to advance, we need our enemies. If the weight vanished, the weightlifter couldn't get stronger. Likewise, if those who would stand in our way suddenly stood aside, we lose an opportunity to develop our strength. Even though at the higher levels of strength we treat those who attack us as if they are not there, we still need them there. Walking an easy path does not bring mental strength and it never leads to greatness.

In the last two chapters we have looked at how the people around us can help and hinder our progress. We have also seen how their effect on our development is not always as it may first appear (e.g. our friends can hinder our progress by being too helpful, and our enemies can make us stronger by providing a resistance to overcome). In the next chapter we'll look at some other ways in which people can derail our thoughts and deflect us from that which would make us truly happy.

Chapter 12

The Lost Art of
Independent Thinking

*'A man must consider what a rich realm he
abdicates when he becomes a conformist'*
– Ralph Waldo Emerson

In this book we're discussing how to develop our mental strength in order to overcome and benefit from all the obstacles that stand between us and our goals. In recent chapters we've also looked at how the influence of others can affect us in both positive and negative ways. In this chapter we will be looking at one of the main obstacles we are certain to face as we move towards the lives we want to live: the obstacle of conventional thinking.

The vast majority of people are not living their ideal lives, nor are they making the effort to change their lot in life. In fact, the majority of people don't even have goals to aspire to. They may, as a token gesture, buy a lottery ticket once a week, but they don't make any real effort to advance themselves and have generally settled for less than they are truly capable of achieving. The big question is why do people settle for the mediocre?

In Chapter Two we discussed how our outdated survival instinct generates mental resistance every time we attempt to move outside our comfort zone and therefore inadvertently encourages us to play it safe. In order to advance ourselves we need the mental strength to deal with the discomfort we will experience when we move outside our comfort zone. And the only way to gain this strength is to start moving outside our comfort zone!

If we want to advance we must face up to and experience discomfort. The vast majority of people, far from courting discomfort, do whatever they can to avoid it. It's not that people dislike change – most people would like to change some aspect of their lives – it's just that they are not prepared to accept the discomfort that always accompanies change, even positive change. We therefore have a situation where many people wish to keep things exactly as they are (better the devil you know than the devil you don't, etc.) rather than deal with discomfort. And because discomfort is a vital part of personal advancement, this desire to avoid discomfort means that most people will settle for less than they are capable of achieving.

The culture of any group is determined by the beliefs and actions of the people who make up that group. In previous chapters, we've discussed how important it is to be around people who both share your goals and are striving to reach their own goals. By doing so, we will be part of a culture that encourages growth. However, because the majority of people want to stay firmly within their comfort zones, there is a strong possibility that initially the everyday culture of the people around you will be one that encourages you to stay within the comfort zone. This will obviously start to change as you advance, but to begin with you are likely to find yourself as part of a culture that intentionally and unintentionally discourages growth.

A collective desire to stay within the comfort zone results in a culture that conditions us to believe that it is better to play it safe and aim for an easy life. If we accept that everyone can develop themselves and change their lives, it also means that your situation is your personal responsibility. This is a responsibility that most people aren't willing to accept. The majority of people are also uncomfortable when the actions of others remind them of their own failure to fulfil their true potential. We will therefore frequently find ourselves in situations where the prevailing culture is one of compromised goals and encouraged mediocrity.

To think differently from the crowd requires great mental strength. When most of the people around you aspire to the everyday it takes courage and a strong self-belief to think independently, to step aside from the crowd and walk the path less travelled. You therefore shouldn't be surprised if setting goals for yourself and then striving to achieve those goals is sometimes discouraged, or perhaps even construed as getting above your station.

In the distant past, when humans lived in small hunter-gatherer groups, it was important to ensure that the group all had exactly the same priorities and view of the world. You needed the help, support and protection of the small band of people around you if you were to survive. The group would therefore encourage unity, discourage any attempts at independence, and would do its best to ensure that everyone knew their place. If the group decided that you were not serving the best interests of the group, they may well extradite you from the group. At a time when you needed a group to survive, non-acceptance by the group could very well be fatal. People quickly learnt that acceptance by the group was vital for survival. Indeed, it was actively taught by one generation to the next (in the form of culture, tradition, etc.) in order to ensure group unity. This tradition of conformity has become a long established practise that still endures to this day. Things are, of course, very different today and non-acceptance is unlikely to prove fatal. However, conformity is still encouraged and as a result a fear of non-acceptance still runs very deep in most people.

Having been indoctrinated into a culture of fitting in, whenever we are about to behave in a way that will separate us from the group, the survival mechanism will intervene and generate mental resistance in an attempt to prevent us from doing so. The problem we face in today's society is that the group, by default, generally aspires to the mediocre due to most people's unwillingness to embrace discomfort and leave the comfort zone. Therefore, if we succumb to this social pressure we limit our achievements and our level of happiness to the average and mediocre.

Human beings are social animals and therefore most people want to be accepted by their peers and feel part of the gang. However, we must always strive for what makes us feel fulfilled and happy as individuals. We should never sacrifice or dilute our aspirations just to fit in. Nor should we allow convention or peer pressure to influence our goals because that effectively means we are putting others in charge of our lives. We only have one life and there's less of it left every second! We must ensure that we live that life in the best way for us as the unique individuals that we all are. We should never deny our potential or our dreams in order to remain conventional.

Despite the fact that a culture of conventional thinking has been around for eons, it is not the natural way of things. It is predominantly something we learn from others over the course of our lives. Ask a four-year-old child what they want to be when they grow up and you'll be told things like a racing car driver, an astronaut, a singer, a supermodel, a footballer, a ballerina etc. However, by the time children leave school the overwhelming majority have severely reduced their aspirations and most are just happy to have a job! Somewhere along the way we get convinced that our original aspirations were childish and that we should settle for something more sensible and practical. Our conventional thoughts mean that we pursue conventional (as in average) careers and lifestyles.

A friend of mine was always very keen on motor sport. In his teens, he'd been lucky enough to become associated with a rally driving team and spent whatever time he could with mechanics and drivers. He was so enchanted with rally driving that he decided that it was what he wanted to do with his life.

When he was around fifteen years old he had to go and see the careers advisor at his school. When my friend was asked what he wanted to be, he excitedly replied that he was going to be a rally driver. The careers advisor promptly told him that he should aim for something more practical and then gave him an application form for the local factory. In less than five minutes the careers advisor convinced my friend that being a rally driver was just a childish dream and that he really should consider a more realistic career. My friend took his advice and applied for the local factory where he still works to this day. His job pays the bills, but it will never be as satisfying as working in the field of motor racing which he still retains a great passion for.

I can't help that feel my friend should have asked the careers advisor what he wanted to be when he was younger. And if he had answered anything other than 'careers advisor' my friend would be justified in saying that perhaps the careers advisor was therefore not qualified to give advice seeing as he'd messed up his own career!

The fact is that people do race cars for a living. There is no reason at all why my friend couldn't have pursued his dream. The careers advisor should have advised him to contact all the relevant bodies and organisations. Speak to those who work in that field and see what advice they could give. He had already made contacts in the racing world and he should have been encouraged to network further. Certainly, he may have needed to get a day job to pay the bills whilst he pursued his goals. So perhaps the careers advisor should have encouraged him to look at becoming a mechanic and see if he could get an apprenticeship with a firm that dealt with rally cars etc. However, in the area where he lives, a job at the local factory is regarded as a great success and therefore both the careers advisor and my friend accepted the conventional wisdom.

As we grow older and become more indoctrinated into mediocre thinking, it becomes harder and harder to think independently. To lead truly happy lives we need to be able to reject conventional thinking and be prepared to go against the crowd. One crucial aspect of independent thought is being prepared to clearly define what success means to you. The conventional vision of success tends to include a big house, plenty of money, owning nice things and so on. If that's what you want from life then that's great. However, we should always remember that success is not material wealth, nor is it the things we own. So what is success? The best definition of success I've come across is that of prolific author and journalist Christopher Morley who said, 'There is only one success – to be able to spend your life in your own way.' Success is whatever makes you happy. It is not about conforming to the prevailing vision of success.

One person I know always wanted to be a bus driver. For as far back as I can remember that was always his dream. Whenever he was asked what he wanted to be when he grew up, he always answered 'bus driver'. Now it may seem like a strange goal to some, but being able to drive buses for a living was his vision of success. Do you want to know where I last saw him? He was behind the wheel of a bus! He'd achieved his ambition. He had a clear goal and he went out and achieved it. I'm sure there are millionaires in mansions that are nowhere near as happy as this guy. Success is always what we personally decide it should be. We will never be happy if we chase other people's vision of success, even if that vision is shared by millions! We need to have the mental strength to create and then stand by our own vision of a perfect life.

Freeing ourselves from the constraints of conventional thinking is a must if we are to be able to live extraordinary lives and achieve extraordinary things. Try to name a hugely successful person from the past or present who wasn't considered controversial, rebellious, crazy, unorthodox, one-of-a-kind or unique. I can't think of one either! It would seem that a prerequisite of success is being able to think independently and in unorthodox ways. As we've already said, it takes courage to go against the crowd (doing so invariably means the crowd is going against you). However, if you dare to be different, you can be sure that although you're walking a path less travelled, it is a path travelled by all successful people.

Independent thought is definitely a dying art. Those who are prepared to think independently often fail to grasp the magnitude of what they're up against. Our upbringing and schooling have encouraged a certain mode of thinking. The films and TV shows we watch, the newspapers we read, the music we listen to and the people we encounter all have an effect on our way of thinking.

From the moment we get up to the moment we go to sleep, we're bombarded with advertisements which also attempt to mould our opinions. All it takes is a celebrity to dress in a certain way or to get a certain hair cut, and in the space of a week tens of thousands of people all look the same. People generally look the way they are encouraged to look, desire the items they are told they must have, listen to the music they are told to listen to and hold the opinions voiced in the newspapers and magazines they are also encouraged to read. Our way of thinking is influenced by a million different sources and it can sometimes be very difficult to separate our own thoughts and opinions from the thoughts and opinions encouraged by these sources. Independent thought is rarely easy or straightforward.

Thinking independently is not about automatically rejecting widely-held opinions and views. Independent thought is being prepared to think for yourself, objectively question the established wisdom and seeing if it holds true for you. In an attempt at independence and individuality, many people simply invert the prevailing views at that time, e.g. if most people value materialism, the rebels embrace spirituality. If, a little while later, spirituality becomes mainstream, the rebels will embrace materialism. What many fail to grasp is that by simply inverting the accepted views of the time, they're still letting the accepted views control their behaviour. True independent thought is being the master of your own thoughts and opinions.

There are some who incorrectly believe that independent thought is unhealthy. They believe that thinking for oneself is somehow bad for society, that it undermines established morality and is fundamentally selfish. Although such people may wish to discourage people from being unique, the progress of our modern society actually depends upon independent thinkers! Without those who are prepared to rock the boat, think 'unreasonable' thoughts and challenge convention, our society would stagnate. I think nothing sums this concept up better that the words of George Bernard Shaw, 'The reasonable man adapts himself to the world; the unreasonable man persists in trying to adapt the world to himself. Therefore all progress depends on the unreasonable man.' It is the unreasonable thinker that has the power to change the world! I'd even go so far as to say that you have a duty to society and yourself to be 'unreasonable' and think independently! Also, if we think the same as everyone else, we lose the ability to see things from other angles and hence come up with creative solutions. Modern society relies on independent thought in order to progress and therefore it should be strongly encouraged.

As for undermining established morality, the truth will always be the truth. An independent thinker does not reject established morality, but they will question it. Morality that is not truthful will collapse under such scrutiny. Slavery, child labour, a divine right to power, and so on were at one time all considered by the masses to be morally just! However, morals that are just and truthful will be validated through questioning and therefore have more meaning and value. The undeniable truth will always welcome questioning as a means to prove and assert its truth. Independent thought does not absolve people from their moral duty; it enhances and increases that moral duty.

Independent thinking brings with it great responsibility. As an independent thinker you have an increased responsibility to yourself and to others. You are fully responsible for your own thoughts and the resulting actions. You are therefore also responsible for how your actions affect both yourself and others. Thinking for yourself requires effort and it can sometimes be tempting to let others do our thinking for us. There can also be a comfort in passing the associated responsibility to others. However, this unwillingness to think for ourselves and to accept responsibility means that we are giving away control over our lives and our own destiny.

As we discussed in previous chapters, our thoughts dictate our actions, our actions become our habits, our habits form our characters, and our characters determine the lives we lead. If we allow others to think on our behalf, their thoughts will determine the lives we will lead. The careers advisor at my friend's school thought that a safe factory job was more practical than aspiring to be a rally car driver. My friend allowed the careers advisor to think for him and as a result he now works in a factory.

As you move towards the life you want to live, you are certain to experience the desire to conform, to play it safe and to accept the conventional. This desire is just one more type of mental resistance that we can move beyond and use to make us mentally stronger. We need to be sure to think independently. We need to clearly define our own vision of success and then have the strength and the courage to stop following the crowd and pursue that vision. We need to dare to be different and to be free of all constraints and limitations. We need to be prepared to be unconventional, unorthodox and uncompromising. When we free ourselves from the chains of conventional and everyday thinking we realise the potential that we all have and the infinite possibilities that life affords us if we are prepared to acknowledge them.

Chapter 13

Approaching Risk

'True risk comes not with action
but with comfortable inaction'
– John F. Kennedy

An inevitable consequence of growth is having to face up to risk. To make progress we must move outside our comfort zone and into our zone of development. Leaving the comfort zone behind always feels risky. That is why there is no way to avoid the feeling of risk if we wish to progress. If we always play it safe we will never leave our comfort zone or fulfil our true potential.

Having established that the only way to avoid risk is to avoid progress, those of us who wish to advance ourselves need to look at how we will face up to risk. We have already recognised that the feeling of risk is a form of mental resistance that aims to prevent us from leaving our comfort zone. We use our mental strength to overcome this mental resistance and therefore make ourselves act in a positive way. This positive action makes us stronger and therefore able to make further progress. However, sometimes the feeling of risk can be so great that we feel unable to overcome it. In this chapter we will look at the nature of risk in a little more detail, and the way in which we need to approach risk if we are to advance ourselves.

The first thing we need to examine is why people are afraid of risk when they know taking risks is a vital part of any progress.

Aside from the fact that facing up to risk doesn't feel particularly nice, another reason that people do not like taking risks is that most of us are conditioned not to. How many times have you been encouraged to take a risk? Now compare that figure with how many times you've been told to be careful!

From a very early age we are conditioned not to engage in risky activities. In many cases this is the right thing to do. For example, a child needs to understand that running into the road is dangerous and hence it is something that they mustn't do and should be cautioned against. However, there is a world of difference between risks that can have an immediate and severe effect on our well-being and those risks that we need to face in order to live fulfilling lives. Unfortunately, we often confuse the two and become conditioned to view all risk as bad.

To help us gain a better understanding of risk, it is important to differentiate between taking risks and acting recklessly. When we act recklessly, we act in an uncontrolled and impulsive manner. We have no plan and no consideration as to the effects of our actions. Reckless behaviour puts everything in the hands of Lady Luck and should we be unlucky, the effects can be catastrophic. Conversely, when we take a risk, we will have a plan to help ensure we face that risk in the way that gives us the best chance of success. We will have carefully considered the options. We will have prepared methodically and will have decided that we can take on the risk with a good chance of success. When we take a positive risk, we take a measured step into our zone of development. When we act recklessly we chance a great deal without any discernible gain.

There is a huge difference between reckless behaviour and positive risk taking. However, as we've already discussed, the two tend to get lumped together and therefore from an early age many people are discouraged from taking risks. Whilst it's right that children should be discouraged from behaving recklessly, they should be encouraged to take the positive risks that they will invariably face when they attempt to make progress in all aspects of their lives. If we always play it safe, we will always remain in the comfort zone and by doing so, we condemn ourselves to leading less meaningful and less fulfilling lives.

Having established the differences between positive risk taking and reckless behaviour, we now need to ensure that we know how to approach risk in the correct way. Any risky situation is sure to be uncomfortable, but a positive risk will involve a carefully considered move into the zone of development. We should never attempt such a large leap forward that we overstep the zone of development and find ourselves overloaded. When we take a positive risk we need to ensure that we plan how we will approach the risk and ensure that our current level of mental strength and skill gives us the best possible chance of executing our plan successfully.

It takes courage to move away from our comfort zone. However, courage should never be confused with recklessness. A reckless person will often have little or no understanding of the consequences of their actions. Therefore their actions are not courageous or brave, but are instead foolhardy and impetuous. It's good to have a healthy fear of the consequences of our actions so long as that fear motivates us to adequately prepare and does not become a justification for staying where we are.

Staying where we are is in fact a far greater risk than facing up to the fears we will inevitably experience on our way to our goals. As we discussed in earlier chapters, most people live their lives as if they are immortal. They have no real understanding that they will one day run out of time and die. They therefore put things off and avoid risk, believing that they can always do the things they want to do some day. The cold, hard fact is that we are all running out of time. Second by second, we all get closer to the end of our lives. By failing to take the positive risks that will allow us to grow and achieve our goals, we face the infinitely greater risk that we never live the lives we want to lead! If we truly comprehend that our life is amazingly short, playing it safe is plainly apparent to be the riskiest option of all!

By attempting to avoid all risk, we face the certainty of failing to live our lives as we would truly wish to. If you understand this, positive risk-taking no longer seems as risky, especially when compared to the alternative of a life of compromise and unfulfilled promise. When viewed from the correct perspective, positive risk-taking doesn't seem so risky after all! Whereas some people will avoid all risk and will frequently caution you to so the same, those who will live their dreams don't fear risk as they know it's an inevitable part of progress. Whilst some will stop and turn back, the mentally strong just keep on striding relentlessly forward.

Those of us who are prepared to face risk will always plan for and expect success. However, we also need to face up to the fact that there is always the possibility that we've miscalculated and things won't work out as planned. Now I know some of you may be thinking that having used the last one thousand words or so to convince you about the positive benefits of risk taking, it's a bit negative of me to now tell you that, despite your best efforts, it could all go wrong! If you feel that way then I'm sorry to be a killjoy but it is an indisputable fact that things can go wrong. There are never any guarantees that things will always go exactly to plan. However, the mentally strong don't expect or even want any guarantees!

The mentally strong understand that we only experience risk when we move outside our comfort zone. They also understand that we need to move outside our comfort zone in order to grow. If there is no feeling of risk, then there can be no growth. If we are guaranteed a successful outcome then it is a sure indicator that we are still firmly within the comfort zone. If there is no risk then the task we're undertaking isn't sufficiently taxing to cause us to grow. If we are truly advancing ourselves, then we are, by definition, reaching beyond ourselves and taking a risk. Hopefully, it will be a positive risk, but it will be a risk nevertheless. If we don't move until we have a guarantee of success, we will never move! We have to be prepared to take risks in order to grow.

Whilst some choose to stay where they are and wait for risk-free progress (which doesn't exist), others are prepared to take risks and make progress. We need to be prepared to take risks and understand that there are no guarantees of success once we step outside our comfort zone. Paradoxically, the fact that we are prepared to act when there are no guarantees of success means that we are guaranteed to make progress! We won't always be successful every time we face risk, but we will always gain an opportunity to increase our mental strength, gain experience and grow our talents.

So long as we learn and grow from an experience then we have not failed. We may not have achieved the immediate goal we set for ourselves, but if we maintain a positive mindset we can learn and grow from the failure such that it becomes the seed of our future success. The mentally strong see strengthening possibilities everywhere.

If we take a risk and find that we are not yet up to the task, that experience, when properly approached, will help to develop us so that we are up to the task on future occasions. It is only when we stop trying that we have truly failed.

Earlier in this book we talked about the importance of consistency. If we possess sufficient mental strength, we realise that there is benefit in everything and as long as we are relentless in the pursuit of our goals. Regardless of the obstacles and setbacks we face along the way, by stepping outside the comfort zone we are certain to grow and therefore the success that will result from that growth becomes almost inevitable. Conversely, failure is only guaranteed when we stop trying.

To recap, risk is an inevitable and vital part of growth. We need to be prepared to take on that risk if we are to make progress and live the lives we wish to lead. We never act recklessly. We carefully prepare and methodically plan in order to give ourselves the best chance of success. However, we know that there are no guarantees once we step outside the comfort zone and therefore we don't wait for the arrival of fictitious risk-free progress. We understand that because there are no guarantees, things won't always go as we have planned or would have liked. However, if we are relentless in the pursuit of our goals, and use our short-term failures as a means to grow, these failures become the seeds of our long-term success.

The greatest risk we can take is choosing not to take the positive risks that lead to growth and success. If we never take risks, we condemn ourselves to lives of mediocrity. Facing up to risk in a positive way is a vital and necessary part of realising our true potential and living happy and fulfilling lives.

Chapter 14

Intense Intent

'In all human affairs there are efforts, and there are results,
and the strength of effort is the measure of the results'
– James Allen

Without intent there can be no growth. Our intentions become our thoughts, and our thoughts become our actions. If we are to achieve anything we must intend to achieve it. Intention is the first cause of all growth and all success.

We can make progress and develop talent in just about any field we choose to. However, the first thing we need is the intent to make that progress and develop that talent. By acting on this intention, we will encounter situations that will develop our attributes and therefore make us able to achieve the things we want.

Whatever field you wish to be successful in, simply daydreaming about it, desiring it and longing for it will achieve nothing. You have to intend to achieve it. Desire and longing result in passive emotions and thoughts. They do nothing to help us. Intent, however, always results in action. True intent is an unstoppable process. When we desire something, we long for it to come to us. However, when we intend for something to happen we go out and make it happen. Desire is a form of surrender to the whims of fate. Intent is an unwavering battle plan that gives us control over our lives.

In order to achieve any kind of success, we need to clearly define what success is (more on goal setting in the next chapter).

If we have no target to aim for, we are guaranteed to miss. Once we've established our goal we are then able to plan how we will achieve it. Above all else, we need to have a solid intent to achieve our vision of success. Our intent needs to be white hot in its intensity.

Throughout this book we have discussed how facing up to fear, risk, self-doubt and all other forms of mental resistance is a vital and necessary part of any progress. We have also established that facing up to mental resistance is not pleasant. If we are not prepared to take on this discomfort we are unable to develop our mental strength and therefore expand beyond our current comfort zone. By remaining forever trapped within our comfort zone we condemn ourselves to unfulfilling lives. Moving outside the comfort zone into the zone of development is always uncomfortable and hence we need some kind of propulsion, some kind of driving force to get us to move. Intent is that driving force! The stronger our intent, the stronger the driving force. To truly achieve the goals we have set for ourselves, our intent needs to be as intense as it can possibly be.

If our intent is extremely intense, if we have an unwavering commitment to achieving our goals, no obstacle will be too great to overcome. All mental and external resistance will be swept aside by the power of our intention. If our intention is stronger than the obstacles we face, we become unstoppable.

As you move outside your comfort zone, you are certain to experience mental resistance. If your intention is strong, it will propel you forward through the discomfort. Overcoming the mental resistance will make you mentally stronger, grow your talent and allow you to reach further. However, if your intention to achieve your goals is relatively weak, you're unlikely to push past the mental resistance and are very likely to retreat back to the comfort zone. If you truly want something, no obstacle or discomfort will be able to stop you. Every successful person I know has a strong intention to achieve their goals.

As a child, I was far from athletically gifted. At school, I was always one of the last picked for sports and was extremely clumsy. At the age of twelve I saw the Bruce Lee film 'Enter the Dragon' and was instantly fascinated by the martial arts. I was terrified by the idea of going to a dojo (martial arts school) but I intended to become a skilled martial artist. Although I didn't recognise it as such at the time, the mental resistance (fear, self-doubt) I was experiencing was a sure sign that I was leaving my comfort zone and about to better myself. However, as a young boy, my mind kept flooding with a million and one reasons why I shouldn't go to the karate dojo that some of my friends attended. Thankfully, my intention was strong enough to get me to overcome the fear, self-doubt etc. and I forced myself to go to my first class.

I can vividly remember the first time I entered the dojo. Years later I became the most senior instructor at that dojo, but as an unathletic child, I was absolutely terrified. The class did not go well! It was the week before a grading exam and the instructor explained that I'd have to follow on the best I could as his priorities lay with those who were grading the following week. I completely messed up an exercise which resulted in my getting the wind knocked out of me. My partner couldn't apologise enough. As the instructor picked me up off the floor, he told my partner to stop apologising as it was my own fault because I hadn't done what I was told (which was true). I left the dojo totally dejected and unsure if I wanted to return.

I agonised about whether to return for a full week. However, my intent was such that in all honesty I was certain to return. I did, and I loved it! At my second class the instructor had more time to devote to me (in fact I think he spent more time with me than anyone else). I left that class feeling great and looking forward to the next lesson. I was still terrified before every class and it was ages before the fear started to subside; however my intent was such that it drove me onward.

My intent took me from a scared and unathletic child to a professional martial arts instructor. As a youngster I was physically weak, but my intention to be strong kept me going to the gym and working hard when I was there. Intention has ensured that I became strong and will be stronger yet. My intent has also taken me from a child who needed extra lessons for writing to an author of many published articles and a number of published books. If you have the intent to achieve something and that intent is powerful enough, it will propel you forward, make you stronger, drive you past all obstacles and ensure that you achieve the goals you set for yourself. If you want something badly enough, nothing will be able to stop you. You can achieve anything if you're prepared to do whatever it takes to achieve it.

Just as a strong intention is the first cause of all success, a weakness of intention is the cause of all failure. If your intention is lacking, the resistance you will experience along the way will defeat you. You're likely to choose not to face up to such resistance and hence you'll shut yourself off from what you could have been. As a martial arts instructor, I've observed countless times that it's not the naturals that progress the furthest, but those with the strongest intention. Many naturals fall by the wayside when their natural abilities can take them no further and it's time to step outside their comfort zone. Those with strong intention just keep on going. There's a saying in the martial arts that a black belt was a white belt who didn't know how to quit. If your intention is strong enough, it's simply impossible for you to quit! Your intention just won't allow that to happen!

Sometimes we know why we want to achieve a certain goal and that knowledge helps ensure our intent is strong. As an example, let's say that your family never had much money when you were a child. That may make you determined to ensure that you always have plenty of money for your family. You therefore have a strong intention to run successful businesses and ensure your family never goes without. Your intent will drive you past all obstacles. Your desire not to see your family go without is stronger than any mental resistance or obstacles you'll face. Fully understanding why we want something will help to ensure strong intention. However, sometimes it's not easy to define why we have a strong intention to achieve a certain goal, we just do!

I know why I have a strong intention to work for myself: it stems from my strong sense of independence. I've never been great at taking orders from others and having the freedom to spend my time on this planet as I see fit is vitally important to me. The goals of any prospective employer are unlikely to coincide with mine and hence I have no desire to pursue those goals on their behalf.

Ask me why I always wanted to be a writer and I've no idea! I've always loved reading and writing, but I don't know why. I'm sure some psychologists could come up with a reason, but, to be honest, the actual reason is irrelevant to me. I know it makes me happy and therefore I have a strong intention to write.

So long as your intention is strong, you'll keep pushing forwards. I have a strong intention to write and therefore that's what I do. My intention is stronger than the obstacles I've faced. My intention has made me face up to those obstacles, and by doing so I've grown in mental strength and talent.

I enjoy writing. Therefore, my intention to write, wherever it stems from, has been vital to my enjoyment of life and my growth. Regardless of the underlying cause of your intent, the important thing is that you possess such intent and that it's strong enough to keep you stepping into the zone of development.

Your intent will get you started and will keep you going when others would quit. Intent results in action, and action causes growth in both strength and talent. Strong intent ensures that you will keep going until you succeed. Don't dream about the things you want in your life: Intend them!

Chapter 15

The Plan

'Make no little plans; they have no magic to stir men's blood...Make big plans, aim high in hope and work'
– Daniel Burnham

We need to set clear goals and have a detailed idea of where we're headed if we are to make steady progress and develop our mental strength in the most efficient way.

Once you have a clear idea of what you want in life, and you've sufficient intent in order to keep you moving, it's very important to set specific goals and come up with a plan in order to focus your efforts. We always need a plan to work to. As the old saying goes, 'If you fail to plan, you're planning to fail.'

In this chapter, we'll look at goal setting and planning. All successful businesses run to a carefully thought-out business plan. All top athletes carefully prepare training plans to ensure that they train and prepare for competition as effectively as possible. Any successful project is always organised around a detailed plan. Likewise, you also need to plan your own development if you are to develop your mental strength, enhance your talents and ultimately fulfil your potential.

The first part of any plan is to clearly define the ultimate goal. If you don't have a specific target to aim for, you're guaranteed to miss!

Before I became a full-time writer, I had to endure countless meetings at the factory where I worked. At first I found the endless management speak amusing. Later on I found it extremely irritating. In particular, the use of endless acronyms made the majority of discussions completely unintelligible to all but the most dedicated of meeting-goers.

One acronym that frequently appeared was 'SMART'. This often led to statements like 'This target is not SMART' (which was sometimes true in more ways than one!). Eventually the SMART acronym was explained to me as a tool for ensuring all goals and targets were meaningful and useful. Whereas I personally find some tools of this nature to be fairly useless, this particular acronym is pretty smart (pun intended!). Each of the letters represents an element that a goal or target needs to have in order to prove useful. Our goals need to be Specific, Measurable, Achievable, Realistic and Time-bound.

Specific

All the goals we set need to be specific. For example, it's not enough to say 'I want to be rich', we need to be more specific i.e. 'I want to earn X-amount of pounds a year'. If you have a specific goal you are well placed to determine which specific actions are required to move you towards that goal. If the goal is vague it essentially becomes meaningless. You'll remember the SAID principle (Specific Adaptation to Imposed Demand) from earlier in this book. To develop our mental strength to meet the specific challenges we wish to face, we need to ensure we impose specific demands. Without specific goals we have no idea what those specific demands are. Hence we are unable to develop our mental strength in a way that will help us achieve our goals.

Measurable

All our goals need to be measurable if they are to have any real meaning. 'I want to be happier' is a fine aim, but as a goal it is not measurable and therefore it can't act as a guide to our actions or a measure of our progress. As an example of a measurable goal, I've set myself the target of writing a minimum of 1,500 words per day for this book. That target will guide my actions (make sure I write each day) and give me a measure of my progress. If I write more than 1,500 words, I've had a good day. If I write less than 1,500 words, then I haven't done so well. A measurable target helps ensure your goals have real meaning. For example, a fledgling vocalist may set a goal like, 'I want to play at least twenty gigs over the next twelve months.' The goal will ensure the vocalist will pursue getting gigs (which will develop mental strength and talent) and give them a measure by which to gauge their progress.

Achievable

Any goal must act as a motivator. It must inspire you to make progress and help intensify your intent. It must also be remembered that to advance ourselves we need to be in our zone of development, and therefore our goals must force us to reach beyond ourselves. However, we must also ensure that our goals don't cause us to strain ourselves to excess; which, as we know, can be counterproductive. A goal must take us outside our comfort zone, but it mustn't be excessively demanding otherwise it can act as a de-motivator.

As an example, let's say that a person who is relatively new to physical exercise sets themselves the goal of running a marathon in six weeks' time. Initially, they may feel energised by their goal but as the days pass they are very likely to find that they are not going to get that fit that quickly. There is then the strong possibility that the goal becomes a de-motivator ('I'm never going to achieve my goal, so what's the point in even trying?').

If they had set a smaller, more achievable goal in the first instance, e.g. to increase the distance they run by a certain distance every week for six weeks, they would have made progress against the goal. This would have motivated them to reach further. Goals should always be demanding but they must also be achievable.

I think a word or two of caution is required here. As we've discussed previously, there is a tendency for people to think negatively about what they can achieve (the majority aim way too low). As someone who needed extra lessons for writing – the only child in the school who did so at the time – the idea that I wanted to be a professional writer may have been branded as unachievable by many. Never let this part of the SMART goal-setting model cause you to compromise your goals or think small. When you think big, you release your potential; you're not fantasising about the unachievable! Thinking big should always be strongly encouraged as it makes the big things possible. The achievability check is simply an acknowledgement that achieving those big things takes time and effort.

Realistic

All goals we set for ourselves must also be realistic. This is obviously closely related to a goal being achievable; however, the check of realism is to ensure that our goals are practical and consider other factors.

It is possible that a goal could be achievable without being realistic. For example, I could write for ten hours a day if I needed to. That goal is achievable, but it's not realistic. I have other things to do during the day aside from write. If I were to spend that much time writing I'd be neglecting other aspects of my life. The check of realism is there to ensure that you don't set goals without considering other contributing factors.

Time-Bound

Every goal must have a deadline otherwise it is unlikely to inspire you to action. You're running out of time second by second (sorry to bring that up again!). If you don't set a time and date by which you hope to achieve your goal, it is very easy to fall into the trap of 'I'll do it one day.' It's important to have a plan, but we need to ensure that we don't end up always planning and never acting! All goals must have a sense of immediacy about them if they are to inspire us to act.

When you place times and dates against your goals, you need to ensure that you give yourself enough time to achieve those goals. Consistent and gradual growth is the best way to develop ourselves. If we set too tight a timeline, we run the risk of the goal being counterproductive as we may overshoot the zone of development by over-stressing ourselves. A good goal will have enough time to ensure we can complete the required tasks without compromising on quality, but no more. Time is one of the most precious commodities we have, we must be sure not to waste any of it!

For a goal to have maximum value it must meet all five of the previous requirements (be SMART). A good goal will give you a course of action, inspire you, and provide a way of measuring your progress. The following are examples of bad goals:

• Become wealthier (not specific, time-bound etc.).
• Beat world bench-press record within six months (not achievable if you've never lifted a weight before!)
• Spend eight hours per day training for an upcoming martial arts tournament (not realistic if you wish to avoid burnout and injury).
• Be more confident (not measurable).

The following are examples of good goals:

• I will jog for thirty minutes every other day for the next four weeks.
• I will write 1,000 words every day and finish my novel before the end of the year.

• I will increase the amount I bench-press by five kilos every three weeks.

• I will increase the turnover of my business by at least twenty percent a year for the next five years.

As part of your plan, you'll need to set both long-term and short-term goals. Your long-term goals are generally the end destination and generic statements of intent, whereas your short-term goals provide motivation and guidance for the immediate issues you'll face along the way. As an example of a long-term goal, a filmmaker who is just starting out may set the long-term goal of having a movie on general release within five years. They may even set a goal in the longer-term of winning an Oscar within ten years. Their short-term goals could be coming up with a strong idea for a short film within two weeks, saving up enough money to buy a camera within three months, etc.

Any good plan will be made up of long- and short-term goals, and a clear idea of what needs to be done to reach those goals. I personally find a good way to start goal setting and planning is to work back from the destination. Start with where you want to be and then work backwards to determine each of the individual steps. Let's say that you wanted to get a novel written and published within two years. Having established the end destination, we should work backwards to rough out the steps we need to take to get us there:

• Get my novel published
• Rewrite sections of the manuscript
• Put the manuscript in for editing
• Sign a publishing contract
• Get publisher
• Submit work to publishers
• Get details of interested publishers
• Finish writing my novel

- Start writing my novel
- Plan out my novel
- Have an idea for a novel

By working backwards we now have the beginnings of a plan for getting a novel published. You can now use the SMART principle to set your goals and form your initial plan by expanding and developing the stages you initially listed.

1 – Seek inspiration and come up with good idea for a novel within two weeks.

2 – For one week, spend sixty minutes each day considering plot ideas and making notes.

3 – Spend sixty minutes each day for two weeks confirming plot development and decide events in each chapter.

4 – Write 1,000 words a day and have the first draft completed by a specific date. And so on.

When we are formulating a plan it is quite possible that we will come to a point where we are not sure of the best way forward. To return to the plan for publishing a novel, it may be that we have no idea of how a novel should be structured, or perhaps we have no idea of which publishers to contact, or perhaps we should also consider getting an agent. This uncertainty is an almost inevitable consequence of leaving the comfort zone, but uncertainty is easily remedied. All we need to do is research and ask. We could buy a book on writing novels, do an internet search for prospective publishers, get a copy of the Writers' and Artists' Yearbook, get in touch with some authors and ask if they can give you a little guidance etc. All good plans require research. Gather all the relevant facts, factor your findings into your plan and then get moving! If your intent is resolute, an initial lack of information won't stop you; it's just another obstacle to overcome. And like overcoming all obstacles, it will result in growth.

Having formulated your plan you should firmly commit to it and regularly check your progress against the targets you've set for yourself. By acting in accordance with your plan you will come up against mental resistance, strengthen yourself, gain experience, grow your talent, expand your comfort zone, begin to live the life you want to live and become the person you want to be.

A plan should be something we use to grow and liberate ourselves from the areas of our lives that are not as we want them to be. Our plan should never be something which imprisons us. None of us can see the future and therefore all plans should be flexible. We should never rigidly stick to a plan when situations have changed to make the plan no longer as relevant as it once was. A plan is a means of getting us to our destination, and we should constantly monitor and revise the plan in order to ensure it will help us to reach our goals in the most efficient way.

Whilst it is obviously important to firmly commit to our plans, we must always remember that they are a means to an end. The plan is not an end in itself! If it became apparent that the plan is not working out as initially envisaged, there is nothing wrong with adjusting it, as long as the adjustments help you to achieve your goals. Changing and revising the plan is not failure!

Let's say that you've been following the plan to write a novel for a few weeks and have written the required 1,000 words each day. However, you're not very happy with what you have written and feel unable to express your ideas as clearly as you would like. Rather than feeling compelled to stick to the plan no matter what, and therefore continuing to write material you're unhappy with, you may be well advised to adjust the plan and insert a few extra steps. You may decide to join a writers' group and get more experienced writers to critique your work. The revised plan may then include the following steps:

4 – Write 1,000 words a day and have 6 chapters to take to the writers' group by the end of the month.

5 – Make contact with the local writers' group on the day the sixth chapter is finalised.

6 – Join the writers' group and commit to attending all meetings.

7 – Spend a month analysing critique and guidance from the writers' group and rewrite the existing chapters to my satisfaction.

The new and revised plan ensures that you're heading towards your goal in an efficient way. While we must always resolutely commit to our initial plan, we must also understand that we may need to adjust the details as we progress. The intent remains the same (get a novel published) but the exact route and methodology may vary along the way.

It is desirable that we adjust our plans in order to make them more efficient and relevant to the current situation. However, we should avoid unnecessary adjustments. For example, if we fail to meet our 1,000 words a day target because we spend excessive time watching TV, or we constantly reassure ourselves 'I'll have today off and restart tomorrow' then adjusting the target to something like 2,000 words a week is not in our best interests! Amending the plan on the basis of laziness is not acceptable; amending the plan due to endless procrastination is not acceptable; amending the plan so we can remain safe in the smothering security of our comfort zone is definitely not acceptable.

Remember that mental resistance wants to keep you where you are, and it will say whatever it takes to get you to do so. Whenever you feel the need to adjust your plan, ask yourself if the adjustment will make you more or less likely to achieve your goal. If it is more likely, even if it will take longer, then that adjustment is in your best interests and the plan should be revised. If the adjustment will make it less likely that you'll achieve your goal, then you should acknowledge the desire to make the adjustment as mental resistance. You can therefore be assured that by sticking to your original plan you'll be moving outside your comfort zone and advancing yourself.

A good quality plan is a must for any successful company, athlete, journey, battle, construction and individual. A plan is always required for any success as it will tell you where you need to go and what you need to do in order to strengthen yourself, gain experience and grow your talents.

Chapter 16

Process not Product

'Work joyfully and peacefully, knowing that right thoughts and right efforts will inevitably bring about right results'
– James Allen

Through reading the previous chapters you'll now have a good understanding of mental strength and the process of developing it in order to achieve the things you want in life. In this chapter, I'd like to cover one final trap that can stop us in our tracks if we're not aware of it. It is vitally important that we remain focused on the process of development and do not get fixated upon the end product. The goal is obviously where we want to be and is what we are striving for. However, if we fixate on the goal to the point where we neglect the process of getting there, we will never achieve that goal.

There is an oft-recited tale in the martial arts where a prospective student visits a master and asks how long it will take him to become the best fighter in the area. The master tells the would-be-student that it will take at least ten years. Thinking that ten years is a long time, the prospective student asks how long it would take him if he trained twice as hard as all the other students; the master tells him it would now take twenty years! Confused, the would-be-student asks how long it will take him to become the best fighter in the region if he only stopped training to eat and sleep; the master replies that in that case it will take thirty years! The student asks the master to explain why he increases the number of years every time he tells him he will work harder. The master tells the student that the more he fixates on the destination, the less able he will be to concentrate on the immediate tasks that will take him to that destination. As the student's fixation on the goal intensifies, his ability to concentrate on the day-to-day tasks required to achieve that goal will decrease, hence the extra time needed.

We live in an age where people want effortless success, immediate rewards and pats on the back for every effort made. If the product is not immediately forthcoming, many people quickly abandon the process. Nothing of any real value is achieved quickly and if we want to be successful in the long-term we need to keep focused on the process, regardless of whether progress is readily apparent or not.

To illustrate how people often put product first and are therefore unable to motivate themselves to apply the process, I'd like to tell you about a gent I know who wanted to become physically stronger. He asked me for some advice on weight training and I constructed a training program for him. After a month he told me that he was making no progress and was considering giving up going to the gym. I tried to explain to him that developing strength takes time and that he would be better concentrating on the process of going to the gym rather than lamenting the lack of product at this early stage. Despite my best efforts to encourage him, he became agitated and told me that it was easy for me to say what I was saying as I was already physically strong. I then pointed out that I had been weight training for over seventeen years, whereas he had only been to the gym twelve times! The reason I am physically strong is that I have concentrated on the process of getting stronger for the last seventeen years. Therefore, above average strength had naturally been forthcoming. Because my friend was only concerned with the product, he would never become stronger whilst that attitude persisted (to this day he's still built like a matchstick man and still complains about it).

As a martial arts instructor, I see people putting product before process all the time. Practically every new student will at some point ask, 'How long will it take for me to become a black belt?' However, only very few ask about how they can improve their training, what additional training is available, or how they can become a better student. Without exception, the most talented martial artists I've come across all put process before product. The grades, the trophies, even winning or losing, were of little concern to them when compared to the process of ensuring a little progress each time they trained. While the belt hunters eventually get despondent and quit, those martial artists who concentrate on the process are always growing in skill and strength and are therefore much more likely to achieve their goals.

As people who wish to advance ourselves and improve our lives, it is inevitable that we will occasionally find ourselves doubting our ability to make it and asking ourselves if it is really worth all the effort. This is particularly true when the product is not as forthcoming as we would like it to be. When I got my first book published, I naively thought that it would leap off the shelves and that the hard work was over. Boy was I wrong! When initial sales were slow, I found myself questioning my work and whether I really did have the ability to make a living as a full-time author. I was starting to focus on the product (my desire to have more sales) instead of concentrating on the process of selling more books. I took advice, and then promoted the book at every opportunity (flyers at competitions, writing articles for the martial arts magazines, placing adverts etc.). Because I concentrated on the process, sales started to increase. However, the increase was not immediate.

Our efforts frequently take time to yield results. This is why we sometimes feel that we're not making progress when in fact we are. As an analogy, let's say that an extremely inexperienced farmer sows some seeds and the very next day he comes back to see how things are going. Because there are no visible signs of growth, he mistakenly believes that the previous days efforts were completely in vain! I know that this analogy may seem a little ridiculous as we would expect everyone to know that the growth of crops take time. However, it is often just as ridiculous for people to expect their initial efforts to yield immediate and spectacular results! Regardless, that's the attitude that many people take on a day-to-day basis.

A good everyday example of people fixating on product to the exclusion of process is dieting. If people concentrated on the process of eating less and exercising more, they are certain to lose weight. However, many people make token efforts at the process and fixate on the product (as is evidenced by their desire to weigh themselves at frequent intervals). When they haven't immediately lost any weight they abandon their diet, naively believing the process has failed, and therefore they guarantee that they won't lose any weight. If they concentrated on the process, the product will naturally be forthcoming; even if it takes a little time.

The strong and successful have a very clear idea of where they want to be and relentlessly apply the process of getting there. They are 100 percent committed to the process and know with certainty that the product will be forthcoming. Because they know that the product will eventually materialise, they keep working at the process. They don't care if progress is not immediate or even readily apparent. Those with less mental strength, often lack the resolve to keep going when results are not immediately apparent. They place product before process and are therefore unlikely to achieve their goals.

The desire to quit when progress and results are not immediate or readily apparent is simply yet another form of mental resistance that can strengthen us if we are prepared to move past it and keep on going. You can guarantee that many people quit just before their efforts would have yielded results.

It could be that the very next phone call, job application or attempt would have been the one to trigger the pay off! We'll never know unless we keep on trying.

To be certain of making progress, we need to relentlessly apply the process. If we concentrate on pushing forward a little each day, results will be forthcoming. Sometimes it will seem like we're getting nowhere, but it only seems that way. Every positive action has a positive effect. Just because we can't see progress, does not mean we aren't making progress!

The growth of a tree is a good analogy. My wife recently planted an apple tree and my three-year-old son immediately proceeded to stare at it for hours enthusiastically awaiting the arrival of the apples! We explained that it would be a while before apples would appear, but he still kept a very close eye on the tree. As we know, if he was to stare at the tree for hours or even days, there would be no visible indications of growth. However, the tree is actually growing all the time! There certainly are days when I question whether I'm growing as a writer. On those days, I need to remind myself that so long as I write (the process) then growth is inevitable. By concentrating on the process, we can be sure of growth.

A good way to ensure that we remain process-focussed is to keep a daily log of the actions and activities undertaken that will help advance you towards your goals. Such a log not only ensures that you concentrate on the process, it can also be a strong motivator on the days where a seeming lack of progress brings you down. Looking back over all the positive actions you have taken will also reassure you that you're doing all the right things. So long as you keep doing them, you are certain to reap the rewards. In short, if you constantly and consistently keep sowing the seeds of your success, you are certain to reap the rewards sooner or later.

Growth takes time. So long as you focus on the process you will be making progress. Sometimes this won't be apparent, but you'll be making progress nevertheless. The rewards of our efforts will be forthcoming if we relentlessly apply the process. However, if we fixate on the product and the goal to the point where we neglect the actions required to get us there, or if we become despondent because it seems ('seems' being the operative word) that progress is not forthcoming, we are unlikely to ever achieve our goals.

Everyone who concentrates on applying the process is growing both in mental stature and ability. Some people may be further along the path than you are, others may be way behind you. Another part of process vs. product is ensuring that we don't judge the effects of our process against someone else's product. Just because someone is more talented or mentally stronger than you are, it does not mean that you are not strong or talented! If we are not vigilant, it can be easy to see the positive attributes and great works of others, and to use their success to run ourselves down. If you ever find yourself thinking thoughts like, 'I'll never be as good as that', it's a sure sign that you've taken your eyes off the process.

It should always be remembered that those whom we wish to emulate were once at the same point as we are now. All the greats in any field you care to mention were, at one time, complete beginners. They advanced themselves by concentrating on the process of developing their attributes and talents. And we can do exactly the same! It is only when we fixate on the product, either our own or that of others, that we neglect the process and therefore limit our potential to advance ourselves.

In this book we have discussed the nature of mental strength and how we can develop it. By facing up to mental resistance and the obstacles we face, we will inevitably become mentally stronger, become more talented, and be more able to live our lives as we wish. The mental strength, the talent and the success all come as a result of following the process. By concentrating on the process – to the point where the intensity of our efforts is not determined by perceived progress, pats on the back, or payoffs – we set up a chain of events where growth is guaranteed and success becomes inevitable.

Conclusion

'A journey of a thousand miles begins with a single step'
– Chinese Proverb

We all have the potential to achieve anything we wish and to become anything we want to be. Certainly there will be difficulties and discomfort along the way. That's an inevitable consequence of growth. However, discomfort should never be viewed as a roadblock. Rather you should see it as a road sign that points the way to your success!

Whenever you move outside your current comfort zone, you will experience mental resistance. Mental resistance is not pleasant, but we need to experience it and work through it, in order to become mentally stronger. As we become mentally stronger, we become more able to accomplish any goal we choose to set for ourselves.

Mental strength is not something we either have or we don't. Mental strength is something we develop by following the relatively straightforward process explained in this book. Now that we've discussed that process, it's time for action!

Put down this book and take a positive step out of your comfort zone and into your zone of development. Don't put it off, make that positive step today! No doubt your mind will begin to put forth numerous reasons why you should stay within your comfort zone. You are likely to be frightened, filled with self-doubt or feel out of your depth. And that's great! Accept those thoughts and feelings as mental resistance, and know with all certainty that the presence of mental resistance is a sign of growth. As long as you face up to mental resistance, it will strengthen you and make you capable of achieving all the things you want from life. So what are you waiting for? The talking is over. It's time for action!

Shape Shifter
by Geoff Thompson

Do you believe that the world's leading lights are gifted from birth or even just plain lucky? In this groundbreaking guide, **Geoff Thompson** demonstrates that *anyone* with average ability and a strong desire to succeed can do so in any chosen field.

The former bouncer and factory floor sweeper, now a BAFTA award-winning film-maker, author of 30 books, acclaimed screenwriter and martial arts expert, knows this better than most. From Day One, this book will provide inspiration and prove that everyone has the potential to achieve their own personal ambition.

In *Shape Shifter*, the first self-help guide of its kind, you will learn:

- That shape shifting is our birthright as a creative species
- How to practise the art of personal transformation, step by step
- That with the right strategy and approach, success is always a choice

Geoff Thompson is one of the UK's most respected martial artists and prolific writers. His short film, *Brown Paper Bag*, won Best Short Film at the 2004 BAFTAs.

'One of the best new writers to come out of Britain'
- Ray Winstone, actor

ISBN 1-84024-444-5
£7.99 / 129mm x198mm / 288 pp

Introduction from
Shape Shifter
by Geoff Thompson

Change your life in one day! A bold claim and perhaps it's one that seems impossible to back up. But this book can change your life in one day; actually it can change your life in one hour; it could even change your life in one minute.

Alexander the Great believed that if you could control your fear you could control the whole world because fear is all that stands between us and our dreams. Fear is little more than a lack of the right information or too much of the wrong information. The right words, the right information, the right knowledge can dispel fear in a miraculous instant.

Change your life in one day?

For those who are ready for change, even one line of text can open a portal to a brave new world and let you see what your fear has been hiding from you.

When I was a boy I innately knew that anything was possible. I felt it in my very bones. There were no limitations to my reverie; I could be anything, do anything, go anywhere. I could be a professional footballer (I was a fanatical player), a screenwriter (I wrote and made my first film at the tender age of twelve), a spaceman (I've been accused of being a 'spaceman' many times since). Anything that my virginal mind could conceive I could achieve. I knew that if I could see something – anything – clearly in my mind, I could make it real. I believed it. All I had to do was board my dream ship and set sail into the great blue beyond.

If life is a great ocean faring adventure then, at an early age, my ideals were shipwrecked and left broken on the rocks.

As I started to mature, the social ethos of personal limitation became palpable. As the time for me to earn a living beckoned, I felt a definite shift in my level of thinking. It was almost as if my friends, family and peers had just been waiting for me to outgrow my school shorts before passing on the bad news, my true legacy; *how it really is.*

This new paradigm rocked my world. I was sixteen years old and about to leave full-time education to seek rags-to-riches employment – something in keeping with my daydreamy idyll – when I got a smack in the mouth from my new best friend Reality; a not-to-be-messed-with, hostile sentry that stood ominously between me and my dreams.

I say reality – I mean perceived reality. One that – as far as I could ascertain – the majority blindly adhered to and only the very brave challenged with any degree of success.

In my case, reality came in the guise of a six-foot-two school careers adviser (the PE teacher in a shirt and tie), who literally laughed me out of the room when I suggested writing as a possible career choice. He instead proffered a list of factories looking for lathe turners and bog cleaners. If I really applied myself, he seemed to be suggesting, I might one day make factory foreman. He was the first of many over the next fifteen years to try and school me in the ways of society; invisible ceilings, codes of conduct, unwritten rules. The intimation was that if I ignored any or all of the above, I risked being thought pretentious for trying to seek more; suffering ridicule and humiliation if I tried and failed; and social ousting if I dared to succeed. Why? Because people like *us* should know our place. People like *us* do not write books.

That's for people like *them*.

Popular belief – certainly in my neck of the woods, the Midlands – was that the world consisted of two types of people; there were *them* and then there were *us*. And unless blessed with membership to the former, you were destined for a life of mediocrity. If that were not injury enough, the world, I quickly realised, was also a wholly disproportionate place; there was an inordinate number of us and only a very small quantity of them. We saw *them* so rarely – usually only on the telly, at the pictures or in the newspapers – that they were almost viewed as a different species. This nominal contact greatly perpetuated the feeling that those at the top were different and their grandiose lifestyle unavailable to the masses. They were the gifted few; silver-spooned emissaries born with a genetic start-up bursary, a baton passed down from one generation to the next. This belief, this lie, killed and continues to kill the potential of ordinary people like an injection of cyanide. It certainly slaughtered my great ambitions.

For a while.

I spent the next umpteen years doing exactly what was expected of me. I worked as a floor sweeper, chemical operator, pizza maker, road digger, hod-carrier, bricklayer, delivery driver and nightclub bouncer before – in my mid to late twenties – something fantastic, even miraculous, happened. Something that enabled me to exhume the buried treasure of my youth: the knowledge that you really can be and do anything. I sold my first book. I became a published author. Me, the working class kid from the local comprehensive, the one who left school with no qualifications and no hope. The lad destined for a life of shop-floor drudgery. The popular media believed that the chances of ever becoming a published writer were next to none. Apparently the probability was so low that it did not even attract official odds. And yet I had achieved it. I wrote my first book, *Watch My Back*, on the toilet in a factory that employed me to sweep floors, and a small, burgeoning publisher bought the rights and published it. That is when I realised the truth (and here comes the good news): there is no *us*, there is no *them*. It's all a lie, perpetrated and perpetuated by the ignorant and the fearful. We are all potential creators and to believe differently is to sell ourselves short and imprison our potential in a self-imposed gaol.

We have all been a party to the lie. We are all guilty of using the *us-and-them* rationalisation as an excuse to fail or, even worse, as a reason not to try at all. We have lied to ourselves and to each other. And we have employed these fibs because sometimes it is easier to hide than it is to face our fears and take our place at the top table.

Three things I know to be true:

1. There is no us and them.
2. We are all ordinary.
3. (A paradox) We are all extraordinary.

Each of us is an incredibly complex organism that has the ability, if used properly, to build worlds for ourselves and for others. That is what makes us ordinary. We all have the same equipment. Not just a few, not the minority, but everyone on the planet. And what makes us extraordinary is the fact that the brain, that five pounds of grey matter swimming in your skull, contains billions of cells, each one of them capable of growing to demand. There is not a computer on the planet that can even nearly match it.

We are therefore very valuable. In monetary terms, priceless. To recreate just your left eye would cost an estimated fifty million dollars (and science is not yet able to do this). How much it would cost to recreate the human brain is beyond imagining. We are so valuable it does not bear thinking about. Not *us*, or *them*; everyone! We are all born with this gift and each of us has the ability to not only utilise this gargantuan computer, but also to grow it. It has no limitations. You have no limitations.

Given this fact let me ask you a question, you billion dollar man or woman: what are you using your brain for? Are you growing it by feeding it with first rate information, or are you sitting at home watching the soaps, bemoaning your existence and pretending that you are destined for no more? What is out there for one is out there for all. If the people you look up to, your idols, your heroes, are living their dreams, then why not you? Because they are different? Because they have the gift?

Let me share with you something very interesting. When I was at the 2004 BAFTA awards, I was surrounded by A-list celebrities. If you closed your eyes and threw a dart in any direction you would have hit a globally recognised celebrity. People who, only the week before, I had paid money to see at the cinema were now sitting next to me at the Odeon, Leicester Square, waiting nervously to see if their latest film or their recent role had won them the prestigious British Academy of Film and Television Arts award. What was glaringly obvious to me was the fact that, like the rest of us, they were all very ordinary. Some were aesthetically beautiful and most were undoubtedly talented, but all of them without exception were ordinary people, the same as you and me. They were doing, had done and were about to do nothing that could not be done by you or me, providing we are prepared to dedicate our lives to it. I was hugely encouraged by their achievements, but more than anything else I was inspired by their ordinariness.

There is a feeling in society that to become highly successful is somehow a birthright and not an attainable goal for mere mortals, as though winners are whisked to superstardom straight from another planet.

I had the pleasure of spending some time with Anthony Minghella after the award ceremony. His latest film, *Cold Mountain*, an epic American Civil War movie starring such luminaries as Nicole Kidman, Jude Law, Renée Zellweger and Ray Winstone and costing tens of millions to make, had picked up a glut of awards. What I didn't know was that Anthony started out his career working on a small but popular British TV show for children called *Grange Hill*. Somehow you imagine that Anthony had been magically transported straight to Hollywood, spirited there by the talent angels. What inspired me was the fact that he, like the rest of us, was once an unknown and aspiring writer-director looking for his first big break. He told me that after *Grange Hill* he went on to work on another popular British TV drama called *Inspector Morse*. The TV bosses were so pleased with his work on the show that they offered him the chance to do anything (within reason) that he wanted to do. A beautiful and very successful TV film called *Truly Madly Deeply* followed. Suddenly he had the Hollywood big-wigs chasing after him and some of the biggest stars in the world begging for the chance to work on one of his films.

He started somewhere small, he placed his talent under the supervision of more experienced players, he went through exactly the same periods of massive self-doubt that we all encounter, before ending up on the world stage. I was in the company of what I would once have called *one of them*, but realised very quickly that he was *one of us*. As we were talking, a man that I did not recognise walked past and kissed Anthony on the cheek. 'My brother,' Anthony said. Then his mum and dad walked past and smiled. His whole family was there. It was obvious that, to them, he was just their brother and son and whilst they were clearly proud of him they never, I am sure, thought him an untouchable superstar born to the role. He was where he was because he had shape shifted to his position as a Hollywood director.

Everyone I saw that night – from Jodie Kidd to Patrick Stewart to Harvey Weinstein – all were ordinary. I knew it and they knew it. You should know it too, because what they have, who they are and where they are is wholly available to anyone who has the wherewithal and courage to wake up and take action.

There is no us and them. We are all the same. You know this anyway, you just needed reminding. How many times have you looked at those seemingly above you in high positions, whether it be at work, in a magazine or on the telly, and secretly thought *I could do that, and better*? It is in these moments, when the portal to your dreams opens fleetingly, that you see your real potential. The only difference between us and them is that they have firmly seized the opportunity whereas the majority haven't – not yet. But you can and, God willing, you will.

Success is a choice, not a lottery.

But you must not make the mistake that I made early in my life, which was to believe that you can get professional results on recreational time. What you put in is what you get out; it is no use indulging your dream for a few hours a week and then expecting the moguls to beat down your door with offers of a six-figure advance and a first-class lifestyle. You'd have more success playing the bingo.

Amateurs work part-time, professionals make it a vocation, they do not see it as a job at all – it is the very air that they breathe.

Books by Iain Abernethy

Bunkai-Jutsu: The Practical Application of Karate Kata

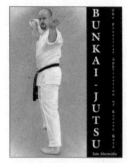

'Bunkai-Jutsu' is the analysis of the karate katas and their application in real combat. It is also the title of this pioneering book by Iain Abernethy. The fighting applications of the karate katas (forms) is one of the most fascinating – and sadly misunderstood – aspects of karate practise. Bunkai-Jutsu provides the reader with the information they need to unlock the 'secrets' of kata and to begin practising karate as the complete and realistic combat art that it was intended to be! This ground-breaking and often controversial book provides a detailed analysis of the combative concepts and principles upon which the katas are based. This book is essential reading for all those who want to understand the real meaning of kata.
ISBN 0-9538932-1-9 /246 x 189 mm / 240 pages
Over 235 Illustrations / £17.99 Paperback

Throws for Strikers

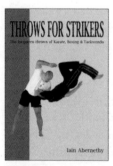

Throws for Strikers: The Forgotten Throws of Karate, Boxing & Taekwondo looks at the basic throws that were once commonly practised in 'striking systems'. In addition to providing instruction on the throws themselves, this book also covers the fundamental principles that apply to all throws, practise drills that will enable the reader to develop competence in live situations, and what to do should a throw go wrong and you end up on the ground. *Throws for Strikers* also reveals where throws are recorded in the traditional forms (Katas / Hyungs) and discusses how throws were used in the bare-knuckle boxing matches of old.
ISBN 0-9538932-2-7 / 240 x 170 mm / 96 pages
120 Illustrations / £9.99 Paperback

Arm-Locks for All Styles

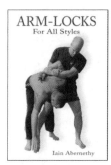

Arm-Locks for All Styles is a must read for all martial artists who wish to expand, enhance and develop their knowledge of arm-locks. In addition to providing step-by-step instruction on over fifty-five arm-locks, this heavily illustrated and comprehensive book also includes detailed discussions on the use of arm-locks in live situations and the underlying core principles of all arm-locks. This book also includes guidance on how to uncover the arm-locks 'hidden' within the katas, hyungs and forms. *Arm-Locks for All Styles* covers locks that can be used whilst fighting vertically and on the ground and is a must for all martial artists who understand the need for skills at all ranges of combat.

ISBN 0-9538932-3-5 / 240 x 170 mm / 160 pages
Over 250 Illustrations / £14.99 Paperback

Karate's Grappling Methods

This heavily illustrated book takes a detailed look at the grappling techniques of karate. Topics covered include: understanding kata and bunkai, the role of grappling in self-defence, close-range strikes, throws and takedowns, ground-fighting holds, chokes and strangles, arm-bars, leg and ankle locks, neck-wrenches, finger-locks, wrist-locks, fighting dirty?, combinations and live grappling drills.

"At long last, a credible and marvellous book on the application of Karate kata! And not one that skims the surface looking for frills and thrills, succeeding to entertain but failing abysmally to prepare one for a real, in your face encounter. Rather this book is an in-depth, thoughtful and thought-provoking examination of possibly the deadliest of arts." – Geoff Thompson.

ISBN 0-9538932-0-0 / 246 x 189 mm / 192 pages
Over 380 Illustrations / £15.99 Paperback

Mental Strength
Made Easy DVD

Welcome to the world of Made Easy! Many people have dreams they would like to realise and aspects of their lives that they would like to change, but few have the mental strength to make their dreams a reality. Fear, self-doubt, lack of confidence, or simply being overawed by the tasks ahead can make many people shrink back from realising their true potential.

Following the success of the book of the same name, Mental Strength gives clear, encouraging advice on how to develop a strong and powerful mind, maximise your talents, achieve your life goals and become the person you want to be. Iain Abernethy offers inspirational guidance on how to break outside your comfort zone and change your life for the better.

The content is broken down into easily digestible segments built around a revolutionary new menu system. The series is designed to be intuitive and to facilitate easy learning, and to allow anyone to learn a new hobby or skill from an expert presenter from the comfort of their own sofa. Each section can be accessed easily to be watched again at any time.

For a full list of Iain Abernethy titles and to order, please visit:
www.summersdale.com or **www.iainabernethy.com**